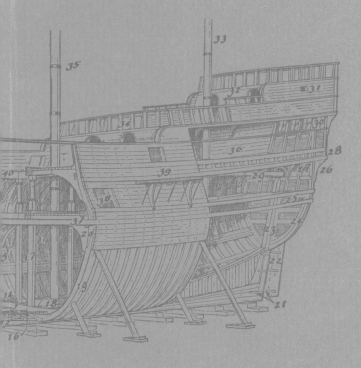

© COLIN MUDIE 1967

6c - 88

A

RENEWAL
INFORM-
ATION

L.32A

THE PORTRAICTUER OF CAPTAYNE IOHN SMITH ADMIRALL OF NEW ENGLAND.

Æ 37 Ao 1616

These are the Lines that shew thy Face; but those
That shew thy Grace and Glory, brighter bee:
Thy Faire-Discoueries and Fowle-Overthrowes
Of Salvages, much Civilliz'd by thee
Best shew thy Spirit; and to it Glory Wyn;
So, thou art Brasse without, but Golde within.

Captain John Smith. Reproduced from A Description of New England, *London,* 1616

A Sea Grammar

WITH THE PLAINE EXPOSITION OF SMITHS
ACCIDENCE FOR YOUNG SEA-MEN, ENLARGED.

Written by Captaine John Smith,
sometimes Gouernour of Virginia, and
Admirall of New-England.

Original published in London, 1627.

Edited by Kermit Goell

LONDON
MICHAEL JOSEPH

First published in Great Britain by
MICHAEL JOSEPH LTD
52 Bedford Square
London W.C.1
1970

This edition © 1970
by Kermit Goell

7181 0588 5

Printed in Great Britain
By Unwin Brothers Limited
the Gresham Press
Old Woking
Surrey
England

Editor's Preface

In Captain Smith's *Epistle Dedicatory*, following, he says: "Many others might better than my selfe have done this, but since I found none endevourd it, I have adventured. . . ." This statement serves equally well as an apologia for my editorship of this book.

I am not a trained sailor or historian, I am a writer, with a writer's questing eye for the interesting interplay of character, action and chance. In Smith this trinity of elements is not only present, but larger than life . . . exaggerated. Also, I love Smith as his friends must have loved him. The combination of the two have been so irresistible as to lead me from my accustomed paths to four years of research in annotating Smith's ten major works, soon to be published in New York, of which *A Sea Grammar* is the eighth. It has been a time of joy for me. In all literary work of this nature the biographer or editor puts in the time and effort because of deep convictions, either pro or con, regarding the author, whom he feels the world should better understand. He is always subjective, with a strong viewpoint—he admires or detests. He cannot be neutral. I am not neutral. I admire Smith, I empathize with him over the capriciousness of fate, which plagued him with disappointment and misery, and rewarded him with everlasting fame. Yes, perhaps I even flatter myself in daring to think that in him I have found a kindred spirit.

Although Captain Smith passed his adult life in the time of James I and Charles I, he was truly an Elizabethan. His training, his thinking, his ideals were Elizabethan ideals, which were exemplified from his earliest childhood by his father's patron, Peregrine Bertie, Lord of the Manor of the village of Willoughby, Lincolnshire, where in January, 1580, John was born. His father, George Smith, was a land-owner of comfortable means, and as an admirer of Lord Willoughby, no doubt held him up as an example to his son. John was sent to a nearby grammar school, from which he soon ran away. Eventually he was apprenticed to a merchant, but because he was not immediately sent overseas, he again absconded. No quiet shore-bound life for him.

If one can unravel the cluttered syntax, flashbacks and confusion of the early parts of Smith's *The True Travels And Observations* . . . , (1630), about 1596 he enlisted in the French army at Le Havre, and shortly after, went to fight in the Netherlands. About 1599 he returned to England, and soon left for France again, this time as the servant and bodyguard of Lord Willoughby's son, Peregrine Bertie, about five years his junior. In France they joined the elder son, Robert, and toured the country. These two were to remain Smith's friends, and perhaps his patrons, throughout his life.

Leaving them in Paris, Smith made his way back to Willoughby via Scotland, suffering shipwreck when his trans-Channel boat ran ashore. Back home, Smith went into a period of seclusion and self-purification usually associated with the preparation for knighthood in ancient days. This was purest fantasy, since the chance of a young commoner reaching knighthood was wildly remote. But fantasy or not, this was his probable intent, for after a course in horsemanship, he again crossed the Channel, off to fight in the "Holy Crusade" against the Turks in Eastern Europe.

Characteristically, he fell into some astounding scrapes and adventures along the way. Tossed overboard as a Jonah by a shipload of pilgrims on their way to Rome, he swam ashore in a storm, and the next day was picked up by a ship which was on a trading voyage in the Mediterranean. Their cargo discharged in Alexandria, they indulged in a little piracy on the way back, and Smith was dropped off at Antibes, and made his way to Rome. Through the good offices of an English Jesuit, he was passed along to Graz, Austria, via the Adriatic and present Jugoslavia. There he joined a Protestant unit.

In the dreadful campaign that followed, Smith established a reputation as a pyrotechnic expert. Eventually he was wounded and captured by the Turks, and sold as a slave. His Turkish master sent him as a gift to his wife in Constantinople. She promptly fell in love with him, and to protect him, sent him to her brother's estate north-east of the Black Sea. The brother did not share her enthusiasm for this Christian slave, and did his best to make Smith's life unbearable, whereupon Smith found the opportunity to beat out his brains, and escaped. He made his way to a Russian outpost on the Don River, from where he travelled back to Hungary, then across Europe, through Germany and France to Spain, across the straits of Gibraltar to Morocco, where he again became involved in a little soldiering and piracy. Finally, about 1604, he returned to England, hardened, resourceful, and somewhat famous for his reputation as a soldier and traveller.

Certainly his reputation was sound enough that he became one of the leaders of a group of gentlemen who were planning a colony in Virginia, and in December, 1606, he sailed on that famous voyage. Jamestown was established the following May, and Smith remained in Virginia until about October, 1609. During that time he rose to become the leader and President of the Council, and there is no doubt that his resourcefulness and bravery were a cornerstone in the eventual success of that enterprise.

The Pocahontas legend, which has famed him but obscured Smith the Man for centuries, occurred about Christmas, 1607. Unfortunately his cavalier treatment of some of the more nobly-born members of the colony resulted in great unpopularity and censure in high quarters, and after leaving Virginia due to the severity of injuries he received in a gunpowder explosion, he never was permitted to return.

From that period, however, he produced two literary efforts of great importance; the first, *A True Relation*,

(August, 1608), was the first account of the Virginia colony ever to be printed; the second, *A Map,* and *The Proceedings of Virginia* (1612), included notes on the Indians which is still the basic ethnological and anthropological reference pertaining to the Virginia Indians of that time. It also included a map of the Chesapeake area made by Smith, which was the basis of all maps of the area for over a hundred years. Familiarity with material in the books mentioned in the bibliography on navigation given by Smith on page 94 of this volume would have made him equal to that technical task.

In 1614 Smith obtained backing for a voyage to the part of America now known as New England. This name was given to the area by Smith. Again, the map which he made was a milestone. It was taken to America and used by the Pilgrims when they settled Plymouth (also named by Smith), who, according to him, thought it cheaper to use his maps than to hire him.

A second voyage to New England ended disastrously when his ship was dismasted in a storm; a third ended when his ship was captured by pirates and he was made a prisoner; a fourth failed before it began when his ships were wind-bound in port for three months. After that, Smith was termed "unfortunate"—a Jonah—and in that superstitious time, that dreaded term made him unwanted on any sea voyage. He never was permitted on a ship to his beloved America. This crushing disappointment to Smith was history's gain, for with his sword and pistol symbolically taken from him, he picked up his pen and wrote enduring history. In 1616 he published his *Description of New England,* a promotional tract for the establishment of colonies in that area. In 1620 and 1622 there followed two editions of a pamphlet that further publicized the area, *New England's Trials.*

In 1624, after more than two years of work, Smith published his largest work (248 folio pages), *The Generall Historie of Virginia, New England, and the Summer Isles.* This was the first true chronological history of the English settlements in the present United States, and of Bermuda, which was considered part of the Virginia colony. It was largely a recapitulation of Smith's earlier works, brought up to date, and included pertinent material by other authors. This volume soon found its way into the libraries of many prominent people, and established Smith firmly as a writer and historian in his own time.

The next year, a further boost to Smith's reputation came with the publication of Reverend Samuel Purchas' continuation of Richard Hackluyt's *Principal Voyages, Hackluytus Posthumus, or Purchas his Pilgrimes*. Purchas reprinted many excerpts from Smith, and praised him highly. He also included a chapter partially attributed to one "Francisco Ferneza," which gave an account of Smith's early life, his career as a soldier in Hungary, and his adventures in Turkey, Europe and Africa. There is good reason to believe that this "Ferneza" was a *nom de plume* for Smith himself. This account was backed up by the authority of Purchas, and attested to by the men in England who had served under Smith in Hungary. Congratulatory verses by two of them, Ensigns Robinson and Carleton, which had been originally published in *A Description of New England*, had been reprinted in *The Generall Historie* the year before. All this tended to remind the public of Smith's exploits as a soldier.

With the publication of the *History*, it is understandable that Smith had had his fill, for the moment, of historical writing. For his next book he turned to the contemporary scene, and with war with Spain imminent, in 1626 he published the first sailors' word book in the language, a manual entitled *An Accidence, or a Pathway to Experience. Necessary for all Young Seamen. . . .* In 1627 he enlarged this into the present volume, *A Sea Grammar*. These books will be dealt with in detail below.

There is no doubt that by then Smith had reached a position of respect that brought him the friendship and patronage of many important people. He had a meagre income from his writing, and his family property in Lincolnshire could have yielded very little. At that time people in the arts—even Shakespeare—were dependant on the largess of wealthy and cultured patrons, who kept a few writers or scholars at their homes, and paid for their publications. Smith's *Generall Historie* had been financed by the Duchess of Richmond and Lennox, one of the richest women in England, who, as a Lady-in-Waiting to Queen Anne, had probably known Pocahontas. *The Sea Grammar*'s publication was underwritten by Sir Samuel Saltonstall, a cousin of the first Saltonstall to come to New England, Sir Richard. Saltonstall must have remained a patron over the years, because in Smith's will he mentioned "my trunk standing in my chamber at Sir Samuall Saltonstall's house in St. Sepulcher's Parish."

In 1629 Smith was asked to set down his biography by Sir Robert Cotton, the greatest antiquarian and manuscript collector of his day, whose collection is one of the cornerstones of the British Museum Library. After a lifetime of disappointments this must have been sweet indeed to the old explorer. The result was *The True Travels, Adventures, And Observations Of Captaine John Smith* (1630), based largely on the material in the "Ferneza" account in Purchas.

One book more came from Smith's pen: in 1631, *Advertisements for the unexperienced Planters of New England, or any where*. This was a peroration of all Smith's ideas on colonization—a congratulatory essay, tempered with fatherly advice, to the Pilgrim and Puritan settlers of New England. There is ample evidence in the serenity and finality of the text that Smith sensed the end of the road. In the same year he passed away, but remained an immortal.

II

As we have mentioned above, 1625 was a time of great stir in England over the impending war with Spain. Since the naval and military might built up by Queen Elizabeth had been allowed to deteriorate by the peace-loving King James I, the conscription ordered by Charles I caught the country completely unprepared. In the ensuing rush for militarization, writers capitalized on the demand with hastily prepared books and manuals. Among these was a remarkably prolific hack, Gervaise Markham, who had produced works on a variety of subjects from horseshoeing to cookery. By a coincidence, it appears that he and Smith had patrons in common, for we find that in 1616 Markham published *Maison Rustique, or the Countrey Farme*, a gigantic tome covering every aspect of farm living, which was dedicated to Robert and Peregrine Bertie, Smith's old companions and patrons! In 1625 Markham, rising to the national emergency, produced *The Soldier's Accidence, or an Introduction into Military Discipline*. An "Accidence" was a primer or manual on the rudiments of any subject.

Page numbers in the original are given in square brackets, also words omitted and added to the original to clarify the text; quotations from Mainwaring which complete partial quotations made by Smith are followed by "H.M." Variations in spelling, common to the time, remain unaltered.

Quickly borrowing the idea, Smith wrote the naval counterpart, *An Accidence . . . for all Young Seamen*, which was registered at Stationer's Hall on October 23, 1626. Although the book was popular enough to have a second edition, Smith's writer's conscience was not satisfied with the sketchiness of the work, for in his preface to the reader he stated, ". . . if I find you kindly and friendly accept it, I meane ere long more largely to explaine the particulars." In 1627 a second edition of *An Accidence* was printed (a few copies exist) but true to his word, Smith published the *Sea Grammar*, again borrowing a title from a book by Markham, *The Soldier's Grammar*, published the previous year.

As we stated, publication for this was paid for by Sir Samuel Saltonstall, a quiet, studious man, son of a Lord Mayor of London. One of his sons, Wye, was an author and translator of note. On the title page of his English translation of the Mercator Hondius *Historia Mundi* (London, 1635), there is a portrait of Smith along with the other great explorers. Wye is probably the "W.S." who signed the dedicatory verse on page xxvii, following, just as his father Samuel is probably the "S.S." on page xxviii. It appears that Hagthorpe and others who wrote dedicatory verses were also related in one way or in another.

A Sea Grammar, With the Plain Exposition of Smith's Accidence for Young Seamen, enlarged, was registered at Stationer's Hall on August 13, 1627. It expanded the text of the *Accidence* from 38 to 76 pages. Except for the duties of Officers, the description of a sea battle and the section from Purchas, most of the text consists of verbatim quotes from a manuscript alphabetical dictionary of sea terms, *Nomenclature Navalis,* written by Sir Henry Mainwaring.

Mainwaring, like many other British naval greats of the era, was a privateer who was pardoned and knighted by the crown, and became a principal naval officer. *Nomenclature* was written sometime between 1620 and 1623. A number of hand-written copies were made and presented by Mainwaring to prominent naval officers and noblemen. "My purpose," he said, "is not to instruct those whose experience and observation have made as sufficient (or more) than myself. Very few gentlemen (though they be called seamen) do fully and wholly understand what belongs to their professions . . ." (note: this statement was paraphrased by Smith in his preface to the *Accidence,* also on page 76 of this volume). *Nomenclature* was not published until 1644 (see *The Life and Works of Sir Henry Mainwaring,* ed. G. E. Mainwaring and W. G. Perrin, 2 Vols., Navy Records Society (London, 1920–22).

Criticism has been levelled at Smith for not giving proper credit for material which he utilized. With Mainwaring's work so familiar to those on the level where Smith sought patronage, he could not have been as stupid as to expose himself to charges of plagarism. Certainly Saltonstall would not have given his support to a badly cribbed work, and one must consider Smith's statement that he had been "persuaded to print this discourse," perhaps even with Mainwaring's knowledge and consent, obtained through his friend Robert Bertie, also a leading naval officer, who became the Earl of Lindsey in 1626.

From a comparison of existing manuscript copies of Mainwaring's dictionary, it appears that Smith had access to the copy belonging to no less a personage than the Earl of Buckingham, Lord High Admiral of the Navy! However, in Mainwaring's *Works* (*ibid.*, II 82), it is noted that in 1697 there was a manuscript copy of the *Nomenclature* in the possession of Sir Erasmus Norwich, with a title page varying from the rest in that it stated, ". . . with a table of the names of the great ordnance, the height of their diameters, their weight, length, etc." This is very similar to the title page of the *Accidence*. Since this copy is not extant, it is possible that it contained the same material as the Buckingham copy, and was Smith's source. At any rate, it illustrates his uncanny ability to have access to classified material in high places.

Smith's bibliographies of books on ordnance and navigation (see pages 89, 90 and 94) are of great value to the scholar. Examination shows that Smith was at least familiar with the contents of all of them, since quotations from them keep popping up at random. Of particular interest is *Master Robert Norton's expositions upon maister Digs.* Norton was evidently a good friend of Smith's, and had written a dedicatory verse for the *Generall Historie.* In return, Smith wrote a verse for Norton's *The Gunner,* 1628 (A 4 verso), which is here reprinted. Today, in this threatening world, his viewpoint is highly cogent.

In the due Honor of the Author Master
Robert Norton, and his Worke.

Perfection, if 't hath ever been attayned,
In Gunners *Art, this author hath it gayned,*
By Study and Experiences, and he
The Fruite of all his Paynes hath offered Thee,

A Present well befitting this our age,
When all the World is but a Martiall stage:
Let sweeter Studies lull a sleepe and please
Men, who presume security, but these
Thy Labors practizd, shall more safely guard
Those that foresee the Danger, th'other bar'd
This benefite: Wee Soldiers do imbrace
This rare and usefull Worke, and o're the face
Of all the World, let thy Fames Echo sound
More than that roaring Engin, and redound
to th' Honor of our Nation that thy Paynes
Transcends all former, and their glory staines.

Captaine John Smith
Hungariensis

Note the adaptation of Shakespeare's famous line from *As You Like It.* Also of interest is the word "Hungariensis," . . . "of Hungary." This of course refers to Smith's service in Hungary, and is analogous in intent to the phrases, "Gordon of Khartoum" or "Montgomery of El Alamein." With the publication of the Ferneza story backed up by the authority of Purchas, Smith's stature seems to have increased to the point where he found it more useful to be known for his Hungarian exploits than for those in America.

A Sea Grammar was a popular book, and was reprinted in augmented form many times after Smith's death. Copies published in 1653, 1691, 1692 and 1699 are extant. In writing it, Smith used his proven method which he had used in *The Generall Histories*—of taking basic material, which in this case had been alphabetically arranged by Mainwaring, and organizing it in a logical sequence. He starts by telling how to build a ship, and gradually works up to the conduct of a sea battle. The book is a treasury of obsolete terms and is quoted copiously as a source in the *Oxford English Dictionary.* A surprising number of modern sounding colloquialisms are found therein—"the bitter('s) end—in the offing,—to tide over," and, "under the weather," among others.

As with most books of the time, there is an abundance of errors of punctuation and typography. Where necessary, punctuation has been altered to clarify the text. Quotation marks, which were not used at the time, have been added to dialogue, particularly in the battle scenes. Defined words, terms and phrases have been italicized for better understanding.

Many typographical errors have been altered, the most common of which is the juxtaposition of *u* and *n*. Others occurred in connection with the letters *t*, *r*, and *f*, the obsolete form of *s*. However, comparison of several original copies of the *Sea Grammar* revealed that in many cases the error was caused by a broken or badly imprinted letter, as *lath* for *lafh*, *shears* for *sheats*, etc.

In deciding where to draw the line in annotation, any word not found in the *International Maritime Dictionary* by Rene de Kerchove (Brussels, New York 1961) was footnoted. No reference was more valuable for running down the obscure and obsolete than the *Oxford English Dictionary*. The completeness of coverage and the number of times where Smith is a principal source was a never-ending marvel. Other books of value were, *The Sailor's Word Book*, by Admiral W. H. Smith (London, 1867); *Dictionary of Nautical Terms* (Glasgow, 1955). David M. Waters, *The Art of Navigation in England in Elizabethan and Early Stuart Times* (New Haven, 1958) was of the greatest aid in tracking down the books on navigation in Smith's bibliography, and for other valuable information on the period.

Boteler's Dialogues, by Nathaniel Butler (c. 1634), was also consulted, but it appears that Butler's principal source was *A Sea Grammar*. This seems fair enough, since Book V of Smith's *Generall Historie* is based mainly on a manuscript history of Bermuda attributed to Butler, who was a governor of that colony.

The editor wishes to acknowledge his debt to Lt. Cdr. G. P. B. Naish, R.N.R./F.S.A., for his invaluable help and encouragement. Also William Fee, the designer of the full scale replicas of the *Susan Constant*, the *God Speed* and the *Discovery*, now at Jamestown, Virginia. And, of course, any study of Smith is indebted to Bradford Smith, who began modern literary research on Smith, and produced *Captain John Smith, His Life and Legend* (Philadelphia—New York, 1953); also, to Philip L. Barbour, whose brilliant investigations are evident in his *The Three Worlds of Captain John Smith* (Boston, 1964). I further wish to thank the staffs of the Maritime Museum Library, Greenwich, England; the British Museum Library; the New York Public Library Rare Book Room; the State Library at Albany, New York; the New York Historical Society Library; the New York State Maritime College Library. And lastly, my wife Inka, who travelled many weary miles and sat many patient hours by my side in search of the obscure.

KERMIT GOELL

Introduction

Captain John Smith's historical fame is secure because of his sturdy endeavours when leading the early colonizers of North America, and his sprightly written and invaluable record of the trials suffered by himself and his ill-assorted companions, struggling against a harsh land, watched by the not over-friendly original inhabitants. But his text book for the would-be young sailor, entitled *An Accidence for Young Sea-men: or their Path-way to Experience*, published in 1626, and its second edition of 1627, and a much enlarged edition, also in 1627, its title changed to *A Sea Grammar*, have received little notice. This is unfair, for they are of very great interest to the naval historian and rank as the first books of their kind in the English language, that is, the first formal treatises on ships and sailors and the art of war at sea. The two books are rare and difficult to get hold of and the library of the National Maritime Museum at Greenwich is lucky to hold copies both of the 1626 edition of *An Accidence* and of the *Sea Grammar*.

The author was well qualified to write a manual of seamanship, for as a young man he had seen active sea-service in the Mediterranean, including fights and ship-wrecks, and later he had crossed the Atlantic a number of times, and in 1614 surveyed the coast of New England from Cape Cod (Cape James, he called it) to Penobscot Bay (which he named Pembrocks Bay). He called himself "sometimes Governor of Virginia, and Admiral of New England" and he was evidently a skilful, scientific seaman. But he does not attempt detailed instruction, and declares, "Practice is the best." As a result, his *Accidence* and even the enlarged *Sea Grammar* can disappoint the casual reader. The technical terms mentioned in the text are repeated in the Grammar's margins, but the text often supplies the minimum of definition or description. It

B   xvii does, however, tell us at least in what part of the ship, for example, an object is found, and with what other objects it is associated. It is possible to follow through the various stages by which a ship was built and rigged and made ready for sea.

Speaking in general terms, Captain John Smith gives much fuller information about the duties of the officers and ship's company. He is a most valuable authority concerning life at sea in an English merchant ship or privateer (and all ocean going ships had to be ready to fight), the duties, discipline, how the watches were chosen, how they fed, the problems of seamanship and navigation, and how to conduct a sea-fight. Of course, the description of a sea-fight is a gem of English prose and has been quoted again and again.

Hakluyt's great volumes have many sea terms unexplained. Sir Walter Raleigh uses many sea terms in his immortal report on the last fight of the *Revenge* at sea. He speaks of the Spanish Armada "who, as the Marriners terme it, sprang their luffe, and fell under the lee of the *Revenge*." There must too have been a real need for a nautical dictionary for the home and office libraries. In 1625 Francis Bacon had published a new edition of his essays, including a new one headed "Of the true greatness of kingdoms and estates." Bacon has much to say of sea-power, summing it up in the words "To be master of the sea is an abridgement of a monarchy." The British nation was becoming aware of its inheritance. A fascinating literature was developing with reference to ships and sailors. On the one hand was Shakespeare's *Tempest*, and on the other, a book like *The Observations of Sir Richard Hawkins, Knight, on his voyage into the South Sea. Anno Domini 1593*. This was published in London in 1622 and contains in the narrative a great deal of detailed information about the seman and his character and duties and how to handle a ship in battle, although in this case Hawkins and his men were made prisoners by the Spaniards.

One of the most exciting archaeological finds of recent years has been the discovery and raising of the hull of the

Swedish warship the *Wasa*, 64 guns, 1,300 tons displacement, ordered to be built for Gustavus Adolphus in 1625 and lost on her maiden voyage in Stockholm Harbour on Sunday, August 10, 1628. She was raised in 1961 and the incredibly sound condition of most of her hull and its contents has made her a veritable treasure house of maritime lore, as it was understood in the days of Captain John Smith. Today the *Wasa* is so well cared for and preserved in her own air-conditioned museum hall, that the favoured visitor can safely walk her decks, stamp on them in fact. When her restoration is complete, John Smith's *Sea Grammar* in hand, he will be able to inspect at close hand her tiller, with the whipstaff running through the rowle to the deck above: the elm tree pumps and the chain pumps: the bitts round which the anchor cables would have been secured (in pristine condition, of course, for they were never used): the capstans: and, of particular interest, because to date a unique survival from the past, the brick built galley in the hold amidships, situated just afore the step of the main mast, with its 45 gallon cauldron, suspended over an open fire and able to compensate itself against the heel of the ship, but not gimballed against the pitching into a head sea. It will be noted the *Wasa* is the same period as the *Sea Grammar* and illustrates it perfectly.

Without doubt, *The Sea Grammar* is a book of the greatest interest to the naval historian, and will give particular pleasure to the student following up the development of the sailing ship, or the slowly improving conditions under which the ship's company managed to exist. He will notice how, for example, the punishment of the boys on a Monday morning or the system observed for the picking of the watches was practically unchanged in British ships a century later. It is, moreover, a treatise which poses as many questions as it answers, and deserves much more study than it has received. As material is acquired by such centres as the National Maritime Museum, some of these questions, at present virtually unanswerable, may be solved. Smith himself is a fascinating character and his reminiscences enrich even the *Sea*

Grammar, such as his references to the Spanish Armada of 1588, to the conclusions concerning a ship's proper proportions as taught by his friend Sir Walter Raleigh, or his comments on the famous shipwreck on the Bermudas in 1609, when the shipwrecked company built from the wreckage such a fine pinnace, in which they escaped, that she continued to be used in the trans-Atlantic service for years afterwards.

One more use of the *Grammar* comes to the author's mind. Nowadays the building of replicas of famous ships is becoming more and more common, whether it be the famous *Mayflower* or the not-so-well-known ketch *Nonsuch*, the pioneer vessel of the Hudson's Bay Company, which made her exploratory voyage to the Bay in 1668, before the Company was granted its charter in 1670. Obviously the opinion of Captain John Smith is sought before reconstructing a seventeenth-century ship and the life on board of her. A modern edition of *The Sea Grammar* is long overdue and will be welcomed by the growing number of students of nautical research both in this country and abroad.

COMMANDER GEORGE NAISH

A Sea Grammar,

With

THE PLAINE Exposition

of SMITHS Accidence for young
Sea-men, enlarged.

Diuided into fifteene Chapters: what they are you
may partly conceiue by the Contents.

Written by Captaine IOHN SMITH, sometimes
Gouernour of VIRGINIA, and Admirall of
NEVV-ENGLAND.

LONDON,
Printed by IOHN HAVILAND,
1627.

Title page of the 1627 edition

TO ALL THE RIGHT HONOURABLE, AND

most generous Lords in England, especially those of his Majesties Privy Councell, and Councell of Warre

GREAT LORDS

Julius Cæsar wrote his own Commentaries, holding it no less honour to write than fight. Much hath bin writ concerning the art of war by land, yet nothing concerning the same at Sea. Many others might better than my selfe have done this, but since I found none endevoured it, I have adventured, encouraged by the good entertainment of [A2] my late printed *Accidence*.[1] This I suppose will be much bettered by men in these things better experienced; others' ignorance may fault it. I have beene a miserable Practitioner in this Schoole of Warre by Sea and Land more than thirty yeeres, however chance or occasion have kept me from your Lordships' knowledge or imployment. Yet I humbly entreat your Lordships to accept and patronize this little Pamphlet, as the best testimony I can present your Honours, of my true duty to my King and Country. Thus humbly craving your Honours' pardons, and favourable construction of my good entent, I remaine

Your Honours' in all duty
to be commanded,
JOHN SMITH

---

[1] *An Accidence, or The Pathway to Experience for all Young Seamen* . . . London, 1626.

TO THE READER AND ALL WORTHY ADVENTURERS BY Sea, and well wishers to NAVIGATION.

Honest Readers,
If my desire to doe good hath transported mee beyond my selfe, I intreat you excuse me, and take for requitall this rude bundle of many ages' observations. Although they be not so punctually compiled as I could wish, and it may bee you expect, at this present I cannot much amend them; if any will bestow that paines, I shall thinke him my friend, and honour his endevours. In the interim accept them as they are, and ponder errours in the balance of good will,

Your friend,
JOHN SMITH

TO HIS WELL DESERVING friend Captaine JOHN SMITH

Reader, within this little worke thou hast
The view of things present, to come, and past,
Of consequence and benefit to such
As know but little, thinking they know much;
And in thy quiet chamber safely read,
Th' experience of the living and the dead,
Who with great paine and perill oft have tride
When they on angry *Neptune's* backe did ride.
He having with his *Trident* strucke the maine,

xxii

To hoise them up and throw them downe againe.
Deare friend I'le cease and leave it to thy Booke
To praise thy labour. *Reader over-looke.*

Edw. Ingham[1]

To The Much Deserving Captaine, *John Smith*

I hate to flatter thee, but in my heart
I honour thy faire worth and high desert;
And thus much I must say thy merit's claime
Much praise & honor, both from Truth and Fame.
What Judge so e're thy Actions over-looke,
Thou need'st not feare a triall by thy Booke.

GEOR BUCKE.[2]

TO HIS WORTHILY deserving friend Captaine JOHN SMITH

The Lighter, *Hippias* of *Troy* disclos'd,
Germans in *India* Cannowes [canoes] now in trade,
The Barge, by grave *Amocles* was compos'd,
The *Argozees*, first the Illyrians made,
 The Galley, *Jason* built, that *Græcian* sparke,
 The *Cyprians* first did crosse the Seas with Barke.

---

[1] Unidentified, but he appears to have been a good friend of Smith's, since he wrote verses for several of his books.
[2] Not positively identified. He may have been Sir George Bucke, or Buc, a historian, poet, and Master of the Revels, who died in 1632. DNB.

The Keele, by the *Phænicians* first was nam'd,
The *Tyrrhens* first made anchor, *Plateans* oares;
The *Rhodians* for the Brigandine are fam'd,
Cyrenians found the Craer,[1] and Creet adores
　　*Dædal*9 [2] for Masts, and Saile-yards; *Typhis'* wife
　　(With triple honour) did the sterne devise.

The Tackle famous *Anacharsis* wrought,
Noble *Pyseus* did the Stem first frame,
To light, the *Copians* first the Rudder brought,
Young *Icarus* for Sailes acquir'd great fame,
　　Thou, with the best of these mai'st glory share,
　　That hast devis'd, compil'd a worke so rare.

For what long travels' observations true
On Seas, (where waves doe seeme to wash the skies)
Have made thee know, thou (willing) do'st unscrew
To those that want like knowledge; each man cries
　　Live worthy Smith; England for this endevour
　　Will (if not stupid) give thee thanks for ever.

Nicolas Burley[3]

IN LAUDEM NOBILISSIMI VIRI

Johannis Smith

Money, the world's soule, that both formes and fames her,
　　Is her bad Genius to[o], it damnes, and shames her,

---

　　[1] Crayer: a small trading vessel.
　　[2] The symbol '9' is the abbreviation for the letters U-S, hence, *Daedalus*.
　　[3] A John Burley was executed in 1648 for sympathy with Charles I. He was the Captain of the *Antelope*, and in 1642 had written a book listing Britain's naval and merchant vessels. DNB.

If merit and desert were truly weighed
  In Justice Scales, not all by money swey'd;
Smith should not want reward, with many mo'e,
  Whom sad oblivion now doth over-flow.
For now no good thing's gotten without money,
  Except 'tis got, as Beares from thornes licke honey,
With danger to themselves. For poore men's words
  Are wind, and aire; Great men's are pickes [pikes], and
    swords.
Greatnesse more safe may act lust, theft, or treason,
  Than poore *John Smith* or I may steale two peason
    [pease],
Or drinke a harmelesse cup, to chase away
  Sad cares and griefes that haunt us every day.
Who saw thy Virgin limb'd[1] by thee so truly,
  Would sweare thou hadst beene one that sawest her
    newly,
One of her latest lovers. But to tell
  The truth, I thinke they know her not so well.
And this Sea Grammar, learn'd long since by thee,
  Thou now hast form'd so artificiallie [artfully],
That many a beardlesse boy, and Artlesse foole,
  Preferr'd before thee, may come to thy schoole.
                              John Hagthorpe[2]

TO HIS FRIEND
CAPTAINE Smith; on his
GRAMMAR

Much travel'd Captaine, I have heard thy worth
By *Indians*, in *America* set forth.

  [1] "Virginia drawn."
  [2] Hagthorpe was a poet of some small note. He was also apparently
a sea captain, and vaguely connected with the family of Samuel
Saltonstall. DNB.

Mee silence best seemes to keepe, and then
Thy better praise be sung by better men,
Who feele thy vertue's worthinesse. Who can
Derive thy words, is more Grammarian,
Than *Camden*,[1] *Clenard*,[2] *Ramus*,[3] *Lilly*[4] were;
Here's language would have non-plust *Scaliger*.[5]
These and thy travels may in time be seene
By those which stand at Helme, and prime ones beene.

Edw . Jorden[6]

[1] William Camden (1551–1623), famed as an antiquarian and historian, was chiefly noted for his history, *Britannia*, which went through six editions during his lifetime. He was Head Master of Westminster School, and wrote a Greek Grammar which was the standard grammar until recent times. DNB.

[2] Nicola Clenart, or Kleinarts (1495–1542), was Flemish. A famous linguist, he taught Greek and Hebrew, and wrote textbooks in both languages that were greatly regarded.

[3] Pierre de la Ramée (1515–1572) was a philosopher, humanist and mathematician. He was killed in the St. Bartholomew's Day massacre.

[4] William Lily (1458?—1522) was a grammarian, and one of the earliest Greek scholars in England. His rules of Latin syntax were incorporated into a book known as *King Edward the Sixth's Grammar*, or, the *King's Grammar*, which was the standard Latin textbook, and tortured generations of English scholars until recent times.

[5] Joseph Scaliger (1540–1609) was a Frenchman, the greatest philologist and scholar of his day. He was the son of Julius Caesar Scaliger, equally famous in Italy. Scaliger the younger spoke thirteen languages, and he was fabled for having memorized Homer in twenty-one days, the rest of the Greek poets in three months, and the entire body of Greek literature in two years. His most important works were chronologies, and it is considered that he founded the science of chronology. A converted Catholic, he was the Protestant-world's champion against Jesuit proprietorship of scholarship and criticism.

[6] Possibly Dr. Edward Jorden (1569–1632), a noted physician and chemist, who had studied at Oxford and Padua. He had been a confidant of King James, and is still remembered in the history of medicine for a tract in which he identified a case of demoniacal possession as plain hysteria. He must indeed have been a close friend for Smith to have printed his witty gibes at his grammar.

IN AUTHOREM

Each Science termes of Art hath wherewithall
To expresse themselves, call'd *technologicall*.
Logicke doth teach what Predicables bee,
Genus and Species,* with the other three.
Philosophie, purblind in the first Creation,
Talks of first Matter's forme, and void Privation.
Geographie teaches how for to define
Tropicks, Meridians, and the Æquators line.
So words of Art belong to Navigation
And ships, which here from thee receive translation;
That now th'untravel'd land-man may with ease
Here know the Language both of Ships and Seas.
I have no Art of words due praise to impart
To thee that thus expound'st these words of Art.

w. s.[1]

Technologicall, a
Greek word
compounded of
two Greeke
words, τεχνὴ-λο-
γὸς, signifies
words of Art.

Genus.
Species.
**Differetia.*
Propriam.
Accidens.

IN AUTHOREM

Thou which in Sea-learning would'st Clerk commence,
    First learne to reade, and after reade to learne,
For words to sound, and not to know their sense,
Is for to saile a Ship without a Sterne.
    By this Sea Grammar thou mayst distinguish
    And understand the Latine by the English.

[1] Probably Wye Saltonstall, a son of Sir Samuel Saltonstall (see below). He was well known as a poet and translator. In his *History of the World* (1635), a translation of the Hondius-Mercator *Historia Mundi*, he included a portrait of Smith on his title page, along with other famous explorers.

Here mayst thou learne the names of all Ships' geere,
And with their names, their natures, and their use;
To hoise the Sailes, and at the Helme to steere;
To know each Shroud, each Rope, each Knot, each Noose,
And by their names to call them every one,
'Tis such a Booke as may be call'd Such none
[none-such].

And yet a *Smith* thereof the Authour is,
And from his Forge alone we have the same,
Who, for his skill in such a worke as this,
Doth farre excell all others of his name:
He's neither *Lock-Smith*, *Gold-Smith*, nor *Black-Smith*,
But (to give him his right name) he's *Jack-Smith*.

S. S.[1]

[1] Probably Sir Samuel Saltonstall, who paid for the printing of this book. Saltonstall was Customs Collector, and the son of a Lord Mayor of London. Another of his sons, Charles, was a sea captain, and is mentioned by Smith in the *True Travels* (1630). He was a kinsman of Richard Saltonstall, who was a member of the Massachusetts Bay Company, and sailed to America in 1629.

Smith lived at his home at St. Sepulcher's Parish, in London, and may have died there.

THE CONTENTS

The Expositions of all the most difficult words seldome used but amongst sea men; where you finde the word in the Margent [margin], in that breake against it,[1] you shall find the exposition so plainly and briefly, that any willing capacity may easily understand them. [1]

---

[1] "In that paragraph opposite."

List of Illustrations

Facing page 65

A Table of proportion for the weight and shooting of great Ordnance.4

Facing page 80

Various grenades and fireworks similar to those described by John Smith. Reproduced from *The Gunner* by Robert Norton, 1628.5

Facing page 81

Drawing illustrating the use of the gunner's quadrant. Reproduced from *The Gunner* by Robert Norton, 1628.5

Copyright

1. Swedish Maritime Museum and the warship *Wasa*.
2. National Maritime Museum, Greenwich, England.
3. Jamestown Foundation, Virginia, U.S.A.
4. The British Museum.
5. New York Public Library.
6. Plimoth Plantation, Plymouth, Mass., U.S.A.

Endpapers

Front: Early 17th Century Ship's Hul
Back: Cannon Parts
© 1967 by Colin Mudie

Chapter I

Of Dockes, and their definitions.

A *Docke* is a great pit or pond, or creeke by a harbour side, made convenient to worke in, with two great floud-gates built so strong and close, that the Docke may be dry till the ship be built or repaired, and then being opened, let in the water to float and lanch [launch] her; and this is called a *dry Docke*. A *wet Docke* is any place where you may hale [haul] in a ship into the oze [ooze] out of the tide's way, where she may docke her selfe.[1] A *cradel* is a frame of timber made along a ship, or the side of a gall[e]y by her billidge [bilge], for the more ease and safty in lanching, much used in TURKIE, SPAINE and ITALY. And the *stockes* are certaine framed posts much of the same nature, upon the shore, to build a Pinnace, a Catch [ketch], a Frigot [frigate], or Boat, etc. To those Dockes for building belongs their wood-yards, with saw-pits, and all sorts of timber; but the masts and yards are [2] chained together in some great water to keepe them from rotting, and in season. Also a *crab* is necessary, which is an engine of wood of three clawes, placed on the ground, in the nature of a Capsterne [capstan], for the lanching of Ships, or heaving them into the Docke.

A dry Docke.

A wet Docke.

A Cradle.

The stockes.

A Crab.

---

[1] Mainwaring, *Nomenclature Navalis*, Vol. II, 141. " . . . when a ship has made herself, as it were, a place to lie . . . in the ooze."
See editor's preface, p. xii, for some biographical notes on Mainwaring.

Chapter II

How to build a Ship, with the definitions of all the principall names of every part of her principall timbers, also how they are fixed one to another, and the reasons of their use.

The Keele.

The Stem.

The Sterne.

The fashion peeces [pieces].

The Rungs.

The Limberholes.

The Floore.

The first and lowest timber in a ship is the *keele*, to which is fastened all the rest. This is a great tree, or more, hewen to the proportion of her burden, laid by a right [straight] line in the bottome of the docke, or stockes. At the one end is skarfed [see below] into it the *Stem*, which is a great timber wrought compassing [curving in an arc], and all the butt-ends of the planks forwards are fixed to it. The *Sterne post* is another great timber, which is let into the keele at the other end, somewhat sloping, & from it doth rise the two *fashion peeces*, like a paire of great hornes. To those are fastened all the plankes that reach to the after end of the ship; but before you use any plankes, they lay the *Rungs*, called *floore timbers*, or *ground timbers*, thwart the keele. Thorow [through] those you cut your *Limberholes*, to bring the water to the well[1] for the pumpe. The use of them is, when the ship is built, to draw in them a long haire rope, [and] by pulling it from sterne to stem, to scowre them, and keepe them cleane from choaking.

Those ground timbers doe give the *floore* of the ship, being straight, save at the ends they begin to compasse,

[1] The deepest part of the hull, where the pump is installed.

2

and there they are called the *Rungheads*, and doth direct [3] the *Sweepe* or *Mould* of the Foot-hookes [futtocks][1] and Navell timbers,[2] for there doth begin the compasse and bearing of the ship. Those are *skarfed* into the ground timbers, which is [when] one peece of wood [is] let into another, or so much wood cut away from the one as from the other; for when any of those timbers are not long enough of themselves, they are skarfed in this manner to make two or three as one. Those next the keele are called the *ground Foot-hookes*, the other the *upper Foot-hookes*; but first lay your *keeleson* over your floore timbers, which is another long tree like the keele, and this, lying within as the other without, must be fast bound together with strong iron bolts thorow the timbers and all; and on those are all the upper workes raised when the Foot-hookes are skarfed, as is said, and well bolted. When they are planked up to the *Orlop* [see p. 5], they make the ship's *Howle*; and those timbers in generall are called the ship's *ribs*, because they represent the carkasse of anything [that] hath ribs.

The *Sleepers* run before and after [fore and aft] on each side the keeleson on the floore, well bolted to the Foot-hookes, which being thus bound, doe strengthen each other. The *Spurkits* are the spaces betwixt the timbers alongst the ship side in all parts; but them in Howle [in the hold] below the Sleepers are broad boords, which they take up to cleare the Spurkits, if any thing get betwixt the timbers.

The *Garbord* is the first planke next the keele on the outside. The *Garbord strake* is the first seame next the keele. Your *rising timbers* are the hookes, or ground timbers and foot-hookes placed on the keele, and as they rise by little and little, so doth the *run* of the ship from

Rungheads.
Sweepe, Mould.

Skarfing [scarphing].

Foot-hookes [futtocks].
Keeleson.

Howle [hold].
Ribs.

Sleepers.

Spurkits [spurkets].

The Garbo[a]rd.
Garbo[a]rd strake.
Rising timbers.
The run.

---

[1] *Ibid.*, 153, "Foothooks: this word is commonly so-pronounced, but I think more properly it should be called 'foot-hooks'."

[2] Navel foot-hooks (futtocks): the ground futtocks in the midship timbers of a wooden ship.

3

the floore; which is that part of the ship under water, which [be-]comes narrower by degrees from the floore timbers along to the sterne post, called *the ship's way aftward*; for according to her run she will steare well or ill, by reason of the quicknesse or slownesse of the water comming to the rudder.

Plankes.
Butt-ends.

Now all those *plankes* under water, as they rise and are joyned one end to another, the fore end is called the *buttend* in all ships; [4] but in great ships they are commonly most carefully bolted, for if one of those ends should spring or give way, it would be a great troublesome danger to stop such a leake. The other parts of those

Treenailes
[trunnels].
Trunnions.
Whoodings
[hood-ends].
The Tucke.

plankes are made fast with good *Treenailes*[1] and *Trunnions*[2] of well-seasoned timber, thorow the timbers or ribs; but those plankes that are fastened into the ship's stem are called *whoodings*.

The gathering of those workes upon the ship's quarter under water is called the *Tucke*. If it lie too low, it makes her have a fat quarter, and hinders the quicke passage of the water to the rudder; if too high, she must be laid out in that part, else she will want bearing for her after-workes.

Transome.

The *Transome* is a timber [that] lies thwart the sterne betwixt the two fashion peeces, and doth lay out the

Buttocks.

breadth of the ship at the *buttockes*, which is her breadth from the Tucke upwards; and according there to her breadth or narrownesse, we say she hath a *narrow* or *broad buttocke*. The *fashion peeces*, before spoke of, are the two outmost timbers on either side the sterne, excepting the counters.[3]

Rake.

The ship's *Rake* is so much of her hull as hangs over both ends of the keele; so much as is forward is said, *she rakes so much forward*, and so in like manner aftward.

---

[1] Large wooden nails made from heart of oak. As little metal as possible was used under water.   [2] Wooden pegs or pins.
[3] The underside of the stern overhang, abaft the rudder.

4

By the *Hull* is meant the full bulke or body of a ship,   *The Hull.*
without masts or any rigging, from the stem to the sterne.
The Rake forward is neere halfe the length of the keele,
and for the Rake aftward, about the forepart [fourth part]
of her Rake forward; but the fore Rake is that which
gives the ship good way, and makes her keep a good wind.
But if she have not a full Bow, it will make her pitch her
head much into the Sea; if but a small Rake forward, the
sea will meet her so fast upon the Bowes, she will make
small way. And if her sterne [sic—stem?] be upright, as
it were, she is called *Bluffe*, or *Bluffe-headed*.   *Bluffe.*

A ship's *Billage* is the breadth of the floore when she   *Bluffeheaded.*
doth lie aground, & *Billage water* is that which cannot   *Billage*
come to the pumpe. We say also *She is bilged* when she   *[bilge].*
strikes on a rocke, an anchors flooke [fluke], or any thing
that breakes her plankes or timbers, to spring a leake. [5].

When you have berthedo r brought her up to the
planks [sic. clamps, see p. 6], which are those thicke   *Plankes.*
timbers which goeth fore and aft on each side, whereon
doth lie the *Beames* of the first *Orlop*[1] (which is the first   *Beames.*
floore), to support the plankes [which] doth cover the   *Orlop.*
Howle. . . . Those are great crosse timbers that keepes
the ship sides asunder. The *Maine Beame* is over next
the maine mast, where is the ship's greatest breadth; the
rest from this is called the *first, second, third, fourth,* etc.,
forward or *aftward beames*. Great ships have a tier of
beames under the Orlop whereon lies no decke, and great
posts and binders called *Riders* from them to the keele in   *Riders.*
[the] howle, only to strengthen all. But the beames of the
Orlop is to be bound at each end with sufficient *Knees*,   *Knees.*
which is a crooked peece of wood, bowed like a knee,
that bindes the beames and foot-hookes. Being bolted
together, some stand right up and downe, some along the
ship, and are used about all the deckes. Some [are] sawed

---

[1] From the Dutch *oberloop*, meaning a runway or platform over
the hold, around the sides of the ship.

or hewed to that proportion, but them which grow naturally to that fashion are the best.

Lay the Orlop with good planke according to her proportion. So levell as may be is the best in a man of Warre, because all the *Ports*[1] may be of such equall height, so that every peece [cannon] may serve any Port without making any *Beds* or platformes to raise them. But first bring up your worke [the ribs] as before to the second decke or Orlop, and by the way you may cut your number of port holes according to the greatnesse of your ship. By them fasten your *Ringbolts* for the tackles of your Ordnances. You use Ringbolts also for bringing the plankes and wailes [wales] to the ship side, and *Set bolts* for forcing the workes and plankes together. *Clinch bolts* are clinched [or clenched] with a riveting hammer, for [to prevent] drawing out; but *Ragbolts* are so jaggered [jagged] that they cannot be drawne out. *Fore locke bolts* hath an eye at the end, whereinto a *fore locke*[2] of iron is driven to keepe it from starting backe. *Fend bolts* are beat into the outside of a ship, with the long head to save her sides from galling against other ships. *Drive bolts* is a long piece of iron to drive out a treenaile, or any such thing; besides divers others so usefull that without [6] them, and long iron spikes and nailes, nothing can be well done. Yet I have knowne a ship built [that] hath sailed to and againe over the maine Ocean, which had not so much as a naile of iron in her, but onely one bolt in her keele.[3]

Now your *risings* are above the first Orlop, as the *Clamps* are under it; which is long thicke plankes like them, fore and aft on both sides, under the ends of the Beames and timbers of the second Decke or Orlop, or the

Ports.

Beds.

Ringbolts.

Set bolts.
Clinch [or clench] bolts.
Ragbolts.
Fore locke bolts.

Fend [fender] bolts.
Drive bolts.

She was built of Cedar.

Clamps.

Decks.

---

[1] Gunports: apertures in the ship's sides through which cannon were fired.   [2] A flat wedge or key.

[3] The *Patience*, a twenty-nine-foot pinnace of thirty tons burden which Sir George Somers built in 1609 in Bermuda, using timbers from his wrecked ship, the *Sea Venture*, and the native cedar. In this ship his body was taken back to England.

third Decke or Orlop; [sic] (or the third Decke which is never called by the name of Orlop), and yet they are all but Decks. Also the *halfe Decke* and *quarter Decke*, whereon the beames and timbers beare, are called risings.

A *Flush Decke* is when from stem to sterne it lies upon a right [straight] line fore and aft, which is the best for a man of Warre, both for the men to helpe and succour one another, as for the using of their armes or remounting any dismounted peece; because all the Ports on the Decke are on equall height, which cannot be without beds and much trouble where the Decke doth *camber*, or lie compassing. *To sinke a Decke* is to lay it lower, *to raise a Decke*, to put it higher; but have a care you so cut your Port holes [that] one peece lie not right over another, for the better bringing them to your marke.

The *halfe Decke* is from the maine mast to the steareage, & the *quarter Decke* from that to the Master's Cabin, called the *round house*, which is the utmost of all. But you must understand all those workes are brought up together as neere equally as may bee, from *bend* to *bend*, or *waile* to *waile*, which are the outmost timbers on the ship sides, and are the chiefe strength of her sides; to which the foothookes, beames & knees are bolted, and are called the *first*, *second*, and *third Bend*; but the *chaine waile* is a broad timber set out amongst them, a little above where the chaines and shrouds are fastened together, to spread the shrouds (the wider the better) to succour the masts.

Thus the sides and Deckes are wrought till you come at the *Gunwaile*, which is the upmost waile, [which] goeth about the upmost strake or seame of the upmost Decke about the ship's waste [waist]; and [7] the ship's quarter is from the main mast aftward.

Culvertailed is letting one timber into another in such sort that they cannot slip out, as the Carling ends are fixed in the beames; and *Carlings* are certaine timbers

A halfe Decke.
A quarter Decke.
A Flush Decke.

A cambered Decke.
To sinke a Decke.
To raise a Decke.

Bend, or waile [wale].

Chaine waile. [channel]

Gunwaile [gunwale]. The ship's quarter.

Culvertailed [dovetailed]. Carlings.

[which] lieth along the ship from beame to beame. On those the ledges doe rest whereunto the plankes of the Deckes are fastened.

Carling knees.

The *Carling knees* are also timbers comes thwart the ship from the sides of the Hatches way, betwixt the two masts, and beares up the Decke on both sides; and on their ends lieth the *Commings* of the hatches, which are those timbers and plankes which beares them up higher than the Deckes, to keepe the water from running downe at the hatches. Also they fit *Loopholes* in them for the close fights [see p. 39], and they are likewise a great ease for men to stand upright if the Deckes be low.

Commings [coamings].

Loopholes.

Hatches way [hatchway].

The *Hatches way* is (when they are open) where the goods are lowered that way right downe into the howle; and the *hatches* are like trap doores in the middest of the Deckes, before the maine mast, by certaine rings to take up or lay downe at your pleasure.

A Scuttle.

A *Scuttle-hatch* is a little hatch [which] doth cover a little square hole we call the *Scuttle*, where but one man alone can go downe into the ship. There [sic—They] are in divers places of the ship, whereby men passe from Decke to Decke; and there is also small *Scuttles*, grated, to give light to them betwixt Deckes, and for the smoke of Ordnances to passe away by.

Ramshead.

The *Ramshead* is a great blocke, wherein is three shivers [sheaves, see p. 23] into which are passed the halyards, and at the end of it in a hole is re[e]ved [see p. 28] the ties; and this is onely belonging to the fore and maine halyards. To this belong the *fore Knight* and the *maine Knight*, upon the second Decke fast bolted to the Beames. They are two short thicke peeces of wood, commonly carved with the head of a man upon them. In those are four shivers apeece, three for the halyards and one for the top rope to run in; and *Kneuels* are small pieces of wood nailed to the inside of the ship, to belay the sheats and tackes unto.

The fore Knight.
The maine Knight.

Kneuels [newels].

8

The *Capstaine* is a great peece of wood [which] stands upright [8] upon the Decke abaft the maine mast, the foot standing in a step upon the lower decke, and is in the nature of a windis [windlass] to winde or weigh up the anchors, sailes, top masts, ordnances, or any thing. It is framed in divers squares with holes thorow them, thorow which you put your *Capstaine barres* for as many men as can stand at them to thrust it about, and is called *manning the Capstaine*. The maine body of it is called the *Spindle*. The *Whelps* are short peeces of wood made fast to it to keepe the Cable from comming too high in the turning about. The *Paul* is a short piece of iron made fast to the Decke, resting upon the whelps, to keepe the Capstaine from recoiling, which is dangerous. But in great ships they have two, the other standing in the same manner betwixt the fore mast and the maine, to heave upon the Jeare rope, and is called the *jeare Capstaine*; to straine any rope, or hold off [see p. 56] by when we way [weigh] Anchor; to heave a head,[1] or upon the violl,[2] which is when an Anchor is in [such] stiffe ground wee cannot weigh it, or the Sea goeth so high the maine Capstaine cannot purchase in the Cable. Then we take a Hawser, opening one end, and so puts into it Nippers,[3] some seven or eight fadome [fathom] distant from each other, wherewith wee binde the Hawser to the Cable, and so brings it to the Jeare Capstaine to heave upon it; and this will purchase more than the maine Capstaine can. The *Violl* is fastened together at both ends with an eye or two, with a wall knot [see p. 32], and seased [seized, see p. 31] together.

A *windas* is a square peece of timber, like a Role [roll], before the fore Castle in small ships, and forced about with handspikes for the same use as is the Capstaine.

Capstaine [capstan).

Capstaine bars.

The Spindle.

Whelps.

Paul [pawl].

Jeare [jeer] Capstaine.

The violl [voyal].

A windas [windlass].

---

[1] To haul in the anchor cable, bringing the ship over the anchor.

[2] Voyal: a large messenger or auxiliary cable used in assisting weighing the anchor by the capstan.

[3] Short pieces of line.

[Note: while the capstan was mounted vertically, the windlass was on an horizontal axis.]

The Pumpe.
The Brake.
The Can.
The Daile
[*dale*].
Chained Pumps.

A Bur[r] pump.

What are the parts of a *pumpe*, you may see in every place. The handle we call the *brake*. The pumpe's *can* is a great can [with which] we power [pour] water into pumps to make it pumpe [i.e., to prime it]. The *daile* is a trough wherein the water doth runne over the Deckes; but in great ships they use *chained pumps*,[1] which will goe with more ease and deliver more water. The Dutch men use a *Burre pumpe* by the ship side, wherein is onely a long staffe with a Burre at the end, like a Gunner's spunge, to pumpe up the Billage water that by reason [9] of the bredth of the ship's floore cannot come to the well. In pumping they use to take spel[l]s, that is, fresh men to releeve them; and [they] count how many strokes they pumpe each watch, whereby they know if the ship be stanch or tight, or how her leakes increase. *The Pumpe*

The Pumpe sucks.

sucks, is when the water being out, it drawes up nothing but froth and winde.

A beare [*beer*]
Pumpe.

They have also a little Pumpe made of a Cane, a little peece of hollow wood, or Latten,[2] like an Elder gun,[3] to pumpe the Beere or Water out of the Caske, for at Sea wee use no Taps; and then [they] stave[4] the Caske to make more roome, and packeth the Pipe-staves[5] or boords up as close as may be in [an-]other Caske till they use them.

The Skupper
[*scupper*].
Skupper-leathers.

The *Skuppers* are little holes close to all the Decks thorow the Ship's sides, whereat the water doth runne out when you pumpe or wash the Decks. The *Skupper-*

---

[1] A pump utilizing a chain to transmit power. Most commonly, the chain passed through a tube in its upward course, and raised the water by means of disks or valves. Sometimes the chain had simply a number of buckets or cups, which lifted the water and emptied them at the top.

[2] A type of brass, or plated iron.

[3] A pop-gun made from a hollow elder shoot.

[4] They take the cask apart.   [5] A large barrel-stave.

leathers are nailed over those holes upon the lower Decke to keepe out the Sea from comming in, yet give they way for it to runne out. *Skupper nailes* are little short ones with broad heads, made purposely to naile the Skupper-leather, and the cotes of [see p. 19] Masts and Pumps.

Skupper-nailes.

The *Waist* is that part of the Ship betwixt the maine Mast and the fore-castle, and the *Waist boords* are set up in the Ship's waist, betwixt the Gun waile and the *waist trees*;[1] but they are most used in Boats, set up alongst their sides to keepe the Sea from breaking in.

The Waist.
Waist boords.
Waist trees.

There are usually three Ladders in a Ship. The *entering Ladder* is in the Waist, made formally of wood; and another out of the Gallery, made of Ropes, to goe into the boat by in foule weather; and the third at the Beak-head, made fast over the Boulspret to get upon it, onely used in great Ships.

The entering Ladder.
Gallery Ladder.

Boultspret [bowsprit] Ladder.

It were not amisse now to remember the *Fore-castle*, being as usefull a place as the rest. This is the forepart of the Ship, above the Decks, over the *Bow*. There is a *broad Bow* & a *narrow Bow*, so called according to the broadnes or the thinnesse. The Bow is the broadest part of the Ship before [forward], compassing the Stem to the *Loufe*, which reacheth so farre [10] as the Bulk-head of the Fore-castle extendeth. Against the Bow is the first breach of the Sea. If the Bow be too broad, she will seldome *carry a Bone in her mouth*, or *cut a feather*, that is, to make a fome before her; where [-as] a well bowed Ship so swiftly presseth the water as that it foameth, and in the darke night sparkleth like fire. If the Bow bee too narrow, as before is said, she pitcheth her head into the Sea; so that the meane is the best, if her after way be answerable.

The Fore-castle.
Bow.

Loufe [luff].

Cut a feather.

The *Hauses* are those great round holes before, under

Hauses [hause-holes].

[1] A ship's rail set up in the waist when there was no raised solid bulwark.

the Beak-head, where commonly is used the Cables when you come to an Anchor. The *bold* or *high Hause* is the best, for when they lie low, in any great sea they will take in very much water, the which to keepe out [when at anchor], they build a circle of planke either abaft or

Manger.

before the maine Mast, called the *Manger*; and a *Hause plug* [when] at Sea.

Now the Fore-castle doth cover all those, being built up like a halfe decke, to which is fixed the Beake-head;

Prow.

and the *Prow* is the Decke abaft the Fore-castle, whereon lyeth the *Prow peeces* [cannon].

The Beak-head.

The *Beak-head* is without the ship before the fore-Castle, supported by the *maine knee*, fastened into the stem, all painted and carved as the sterne, and of great use as well for the grace and countenance of the ship, as a place for men to ease themselves in.[1] To it is fastened the coller [collar] of the maine stay, and the fore tacks there brought aboord; also the *standing*[2] for rigging and trimming the spretesaile geare. Under the midest of it is the *Combe*,

Combe.

which is a little peece of wood with two holes in it, to bring the fore tacks aboard.

Bit[t]s.
Crospeece
[crosspiece].

The *Bits* are two great peeces of timber, and the *Crospeece* goeth thorow them. They are ordinarily placed abaft the Manger in the ship's loofe [luff], to belay the Cable thereto when you ride at Anchor. Their lower parts are fastened to the *Riders* [see p. 5], but the middle part in great ships are bolted to two great beames crosse to the Bowes; and yet in extraordinary stormes we are glad to make fast the Cable to the maine Mast for strengthning of the Bits and safety of the Bowes, which have in great stormes beene torne from the ships.

David [davit].

The *David* is a short peece of timber, at the end [11] whereof in a notch they hang a blocke in a strap, called

---

[1] This is the derivation of *head*, the sailor's term for a latrine.
[2] This could refer to the standing lifts or blocks, but in this case, to a place or plank on which men could stand.

the *Fish-block*, by which they hale up the flook [fluke] of the Anchor to the Ship's bow. It is put out betwixt the Cat and the Loufe, and to be removed when you please. The *Cat* is also a short peece of timber aloft right over the Hawse. In the end it hath two shivers in a blocke, wherein is reeved a Rope to which is fastned a great hooke of Iron [the fish hook], to trice up the Anchor from the Hawse to the top of the fore-castle.

A *Bulks head* is like a seeling [sealing] or a wall of boords thwart the Ship, as the Gunroome, the great Cabin, the bread roome, the quarter Decke, or any other such division; but them which doth make close the fore-castle and the halfe Decke, the Mariners call the *Cubbridge heads*, wherein are placed murtherers[2]; and abaft, Falcons, Falconets or Rabinits[3], to cleare the Decks fore and aft, so well as upon the ship's sides to defend the ship and offend an enemy. *Sockets* are the holes wherein the pintels of the murderers or fowlers goe into. The hollow arching betwixt the lower part of the Gallery and the Transome is called the *lower Counter*; the *upper Counter* is from the Gallery to the arch of the round house, and the *Brackets* are little carved knees to support the Galleries.

The *Stearage roome* is before the *great Cabin*, where he that steareth the ship doth alwaies stand. Before him is a square box nailed together with wooden pinnese, called a *Bittacle*, because iron nailes would attract the Compasse. This is built so close, that the Lampe or Candle only sheweth light to the stearage. And in it alwaies stands the Compasse, which every one knowes is a round box, and in the midst of the bottome, a sharp pin called a *Center*, whereon the *Fly* [card] doth play, which is a round peece of pace-boord [pasteboard], with a small wyer [wire] under

Fish-block.

Cat.[1]

A Bulkes head [bulkhead].

Cubbridge head.

Sockets.

Lower Counter.
Upper Counter.
Brackets.
The Stearage [steerage].
Great Cabin.
Bittacle, [binnacle].
The Compasse. [*Here Smith enlarges from his own knowledge.*]

[1] More properly the *cat* was the cat rope, and this the cat-head.
[2], [3] Murderer: a small anti-personnel cannon, which was breech-loaded. Those following are also anti-personnel, used in boarding and to repel boarders. [See Chart, (page 90) below.] The fowler was a similar weapon, but muzzle loading.

it touched with the Load-stone. In the midst of it is a little brasse Cap that doth keepe it levell upon the Center. On the upper part is painted 32 points of the Compasse, covered with glasse to keepe it from dust, breaking, or the wind. This Box doth hang in two or three [12] brasse circles [gimbal rings], so fixed, they give such way to the moving of the Ship, that still the Box will stand *A darke* steady. There is also a *darke Compasse*, and a *Compasse* *Compasse.* *for the variation*; yet they are but as the other, onely the *A compasse for* *darke Compasse* hath the points blacke and white,[1] and the *Variation.* other onely touched [marked] for the true North and South.

The Travas Upon the Bittacle is also the Travas, which is a little *[traverse board].* round boord full of holes upon lines like the Compasse, upon which, by the removing [the repeated moving] of a little sticke, they keepe an account how many *glasses* (which are but halfe houres) they steare upon every point.

The Whip-staffe. The *Whip-staffe* is that peece of wood, like a strong staffe, the Stearsman or Helmesman hath alwaies in his *The Rowle [roll].* hand, going thorow the *Rowle*,[2] and then made fast to the *The Tiller.* Tiller with a Ring. The *Tiller* is a strong peece of wood *Rudder.* made fast to the *Rudder*, which is a great timber somewhat like a Planke, made according to the burthen[3] of the ship, and hung at the sterne upon hookes and hinges *Pintels.* they call *Pintels* and *Gudgions*, or *Rudder-irons*. The *Gudgions* Tiller playeth in the Gunroome[4] over the Ordnances, *[gudgeons] or* [actuated] by the Whip-staffe, whereby the Rudder is so *Rudder-Irons.* turned to and fro as the Helmesman pleaseth; and the *The Gun-roome.* *Cat holes* are over the Ports, right [as in line] with the *Catholes.* Capstaine as they can [make them], to heave the Ship

---

[1] *Ibid.*, 129. " . . . to be seen when we steer by night without any light."

[2] An axle fixed to the deck of the steerage room, upon which the whipstaff pivoted.

[3] Burden: ship's carrying capacity expressed in tons.

[4] The gun room usually was an officers' mess room, or was used for the gunner's supplies. It appears from this that ordnance was also mounted in this room to fire aft.

14

a-sterne by a Cable, or a Hauser called a *sterne-fast*. On each side the Stearage roome are divers Cabins, as also in the great Cabin, the quarter Decke and the round house, with many convenient seates or Lockers to put any thing in, as in little Cupberts [cupboards].

Lockers.

The *Bread-roome* is commonly under the Gun-roome, well dried or plated. The *Cook-roome* where they dresse their victuall may bee placed in divers places of the Ship, as sometimes in the Hould, but that oft spoileth the victuall by reason of the heat; but commonly in Merchantmen it is in the Fore-castle, especially being contrived in [fitted with] Fornaces [furnaces or stove]. Besides, in a chase their Sterne is that part of the ship they most use in [a] fight (but in a man of warre they fight most with their Prow), and it is very troublesome to the use [13] of his Ordnance, and very dangerous lying over the Powder-roome. Some doe place it over the Hatches way, but that, as the Steward's roome, are ever to be contrived according to the Ship's imploiment, etc.

The Bread-roome.
Cooke-roome.

Sterne.

Calking is beating Okum into every seame, or betwixt planke and planke, and *Okum* is old Ropes torne in peeces, like Towze Match,[1] or Hurds of Flax;[2] which being close beat into every seame with a *calking Iron* and a *Mallet* (which is a hammer of wood, and an iron chissell), being well *payed* [smeared] over with hot pitch, doth make her more tight than it is possible by joyning Planke to Planke.

Calking
[caulking].
Okum.
Calking-Iron.

Paying.

Graving is onely [used] under water—a white mixture of Tallow, Sope and Brimstone, or Train-oile,[3] Rosin and Brimstone boiled together, is the best to preserve her calking and make her glib or slippery to passe the water,

Graving.

---

[1] Gun-match or slow-match, made of teased hemp or other fibrous material.
[2] The coarser parts of flax or hemp, separated in hackling or combing. OED.
[3] Whale, seal, or fish oil, including fish-liver-oil.

Barnacles, or
Wormes.

and when it is decayed by weeds, or *Barnacles*; which is a kinde of fish like a long red worme [which] will eat thorow all the Plankes if she be not *sheathed*, which is as casing the Hull under water with Tar and Haire, close covered over with thin boords fast nailed to the Hull, which though the Worme pierce, shee cannot endure the Tar.

Broming
[brooming] or
Breaming.
Careene.

Breaming her is but washing or burning of all the filth with reeds or broome,[1] either in a dry dock or upon her *Careene*; which is to make her so light, as you may bring her to lye on the one side so much as may be, in the calmest water you can, but take heed you overset her not. And this is the best way to Breame Ships of great burthen, or those have but 4 sharpe Flores,[2] for feare of brusing or oversetting.

Parsling
[parcelling].

Parsling is most used upon the Decks and halfe Decks, which is to take a list [a strip] of Canvas so long as the seame is you would parsell, being first well calked, then powre hot pitch upon it, and it will keepe out the water from passing the seames.

There remaines nothing now as I can remember to the building the Hull of a Ship, nor the definition of her most proper tearmes, but onely seeling [sealing] the Cabins and such other parts as you please; and to bind an end with all things fitting for the Sea, as you may reade in the Covenants betwixt the Carpenter and the Owner, which are thus: [14]

Notes for a
Covenant
betweene the
Carpenter and
the Owner.

If you would have a Ship built of 400 Tuns, she requires a planke of 4 inches; if 300 Tuns, 3 inches; small Ships, 2 inches, but none lesse. For clamps, middle bands and sleepers, they be all of six inch planke, for

[1] A shrub common to England and Europe. The term also applied to any stiff shrub used for making brooms.
[2] Mainwaring, *op. cit.* II, 117, *sic*, ". . . have but one small floor, and are built so sharp under water. . . ."

16

binding within; the rest for the sparring up of the workes, of square three inch planke.

Lay the beames of the Orlope, if she be 400 Tuns, at ten foot deepe in [the] howle, and all the beames to be bound with two knees at each end, and a standard knee[1] at every beame's end upon the Orlope. All the Orlope to be laid with square three inch planke, and all the plankes to be tree-nailed to the beames.

Six foot would be betweene the beames of the Deck and Orlope; and ten ports on each side upon the lower Orlope. All the binding between them should bee with three inch or two inch planke; and the upper Decke should bee laid with so many beames as are fitting, with knees to bind them, laying that Decke with spruce Deale [boards] of thirty foot long, the sap cut off, and two inches thicke, for it is better than any other.

Then for the Captaine's Cabben or great Cabben, the Stearage, the halfe Decke, the Round house, the Forecastle; and *to binde an end with the Capsterne and all things fitting for the Sea*[2] (the Smith's worke, the carving, joyning and painting excepted), [these] are the principall things I remember to be observed.

For a *Charter-party*[3] betwixt the Merchant, the Master and the Owner, you have Presidents [precedents] of all sorts in most Scriveners' shops [public scribes]. [15]

---

[1] Standing knee, which was inverted.
[2] A nautical colloquialism meaning "to conclude."
[3] The charter agreement. For an example of one, see Susan Kingsbury, *The Records of the Virginia Company of London*, Washington (1903–35), III, 381.

Chapter III

How to proportion the Masts and Yards for a Ship by her Beame and Keele

A Ship over-
masted.

When a ship is built she should be masted, wherein is a great deale of experience to be used, so well as art; for if you overmast her either in length or bignesse, she will lie too much downe by a wind, and labour too much a-hull,

Taunt-masted.
Under-masted.

and that is called a *Taunt-mast*; but if either too small or too short, she us *under masted* or *low masted,* and cannot beare so great a saile as should give her her true way. For a man of warre, a well ordered Taunt-mast is best, but for a long voyage, a short Mast will beare more Canvasse, and is lesse subject to beare by the boord [break and fall overboard]. Their Rules are divers, because no Artist can build a Ship so truly to proportion, neither set her Masts, but by the triall of her condition they may bee impayred or amended.

An example.

Suppose a Ship of 300 Tunnes be 29 foot at the Beame. If her maine Mast be 24 inches diameter, the length of it must be 24 yards, for every inch in thicknesse is allowed a yard in length; and the fore Mast 22 inches in thicknesse must bee 22 yards in length. Your Bowle spret both in length and thicknesse must bee equall to the fore Mast. The Misen [mizzen], 17 yards in length and 17 inches diameter.

The rule most
used.

But the Rule most used is to take the 4/5 parts of the bredth of the Ship and multiply that by three, [which] will give you so many foot as your maine Mast should

bee in length; [and] the bignesse or thicknesse will beare
[on] it also, allowing an inch for a yard; but if it be a
made *Mast*, that is, greater than one Tree, it must be
more. For example, suppose the Ship's bredth 30 foot:
foure fift[h]s of 30 foot are 24 foot, so you [16] finde the
maine Mast must be 24 yards long, for every yard is
3 foot, and 24 inches thorow, allowing an inch to every
yard.

A made Mast, or an arme[d] Mast.

The fore Mast is to be in length 4/5 of the maine Mast,
which will be 20 yards, wanting one 4/5 part of a yard,
and 20 inches thorow. The Boultspret must ever bee
equall with the fore Mast. The misen Mast, halfe the
length of the maine Mast, which will be 12 yards long,
and 12 inches diameter. Now as you take the proportion
of the Masts from the Beame or bredth of the Ship, so
doe you the length of the yards from the Keele.

These Masts have each their *steps*[1] in the Ship, and
their *Partners* at every Decke, where thorow they passe
to the Keele; [these] being strong timbers bolted to the
Beams, incircling the Masts to keep them steady in their
steps, fast wedged for rowling [rolling]. Yet some Ships
will not saile so well as when it doth play a little, but that
is very dangerous in foule weather.

The Steps.
Partners.

Their *Cotes* are peeces of tarred Canvas, or a *Tarpawling*, put about them and the Rudder to keepe the
water out. At the top of the fore Mast and maine Mast
are spliced *cheeks*, or thicke clamps of wood, thorow which
are in each two holes called the *Hounds*, wherein the *Tyes*
doe runne to hoise [hoist] the yards; but the top Mast
hath but one hole or hound, and one tye. Every Mast also
hath a *Cap* if a top, which is a peece of square timber with
a round hole in it to receive the top Masts or Flag staffe,
to keepe them steady and strong lest they be borne by the
boord in a stiffe gale.

Cotes [coats].
*Tarpawling
[tarpaulin].*
Cheeks.
The Hounds.

The Cap.

The *Crosse-trees* are also at the head of the Masts, one

Crosse-trees.

[1] That place or seat upon which the masts or capstan are set.

Tressel-
[trestle-] trees.

let into another crosse, and strongly bolted with the Tressell trees to keepe up the top Masts which are fastened in them; and those are at the tops of each Mast.

All the Masts stand upright but the Boulspret, which lyeth along over the Beak-head, and that timber it resteth on is called the *Pillow*.

Pillow.
An example of
the Yards by
the Keele.

Now for the yards. Suppose the ship be 76 foot at the Keele. Her maine yard must be 21 yards in length, and in thicknesse but 17 inches; the fore yard 19 yards long, and 15 inches diameter, or thick; the spret-saile Yard 16 [17] yards long, and but nine inches thicke; and your Misen-yard so long as the Mast. The top yards beares halfe proportion to the maine and fore yard, and the top gallants the halfe to them, but this rule is not absolute; for if your Masts be taunt, your yards must be the shorter; if a low Mast, the longer. But this is supposed the best: to have the maine Yard 5/6 parts of her Keele in length; the top Yard 3/7 of the maine Yard; and the maine Yard for bignesse, 3/4 parts of an inch for a yard in length. The length of the fore Yard, 4/5 of the maine Yard, the Crossejacke Yard [see p. 21] and Spretsaile Yard to be of a [equal] length; but you must allow the Misen Yard and Spretsaile Yard 1/2 inch of thicknesse to a yard in length.

But to give a true Arithmeticall and Geometricall proportion for the building of all sorts of Ships, were they all built after one mould—as also their Masts, Yards, Cables, Cordage and Sailes—were all the stuffe of like goodnesse, a methodicall rule, as you see, might bee projected; but their lengths, bredths, depths, rakes and burthens are so variable and different, that nothing but experiences can possibly teach it.

Chapter IIII

The names of all the Masts, Tops and Yards belonging to a Ship

The *Boul-spret* [bowsprit], the *Spretsaile* [spritsail] *yard*, the *Spretsaile top-mast*, the *Spretsaile top saile yard*. The *fore Mast*, the *fore yard*, the *fore top mast*, the *fore top-saile yard*, the *fore top gallant Mast*, the *fore top gallant saile yard*. *Cotes*, *Wouldings* [wooldings],¹ *Gromits* [grommets], and *Staples* for all yards.

The *maine Mast*, the *maine Yard*, the *maine Top*. The [18] *maine top Mast*, the *maine top-saile Yard*. The *top gallant Mast*, the *maine top gallant saile Yard*. The *Trucke* is a square peece of wood at the top wherein you put the *Flag-staffe*. The *Misen*, the *Misen Yard*, the *Misen top Mast*, the *Misen top saile yard*. The *Crosse Jacke* [cro'jack].² In great ships they have two *Misens*, the latter is called the *Bonaventure Misen*.

A *Jury Mast*: that is when a Mast is borne by the boord, with Yards, Roofes, Trees [sic; roof-trees] or what they can, spliced or fished³ together, they make a *Jury-mast*, *woulding* or binding them with ropes fast triced together with handspikes, as they use to would or binde any Mast or Yard.

---

¹ Coats and wooldings were tarred canvas and bindings around a fished (see below) or spliced mast or yard, to reenforce it.
² The bare yard to which was attached the sheets of the Mizzen topsail.
³ To strengthen a cracked mast or yard by fastening external supports of wood, in the manner of splints.

Chapter V

How all the Tackling and Rigging of a Ship is made fast one to another, with their names, and the reasons of their use

Riggage or Cordage.
A Mast well rigged.
A Yard well rigged.
Over rigged.

All Masts have staies except one.

A Coller [collar].

The *rigging* [of] a Ship is all the *Ropes* or *Cordage* belonging to the Masts and Yards; and it is proper to say *The Mast is well rigged*, or, *The Yard is well rigged*; that is, when all the Ropes are well sised [sized] to a true proportion of her burthen. We say also, when they are too many or too great, *Shee is over-rigged*, and doth much wrong a Ship in her Sailing; for a small waight aloft is much more in that nature than a much greater below, and the more upright any Ship goeth, the better she saileth.

All the Masts, Top-masts and Flag-staves [staffs] have staies, excepting the Spretsaile-top Mast. The maine Mast's stay is made fast by a Lannier [see below] to a *Coller*, which is a great Rope that comes about the head and Boulspret; the other end to the head of the maine Mast. The maine top-Mast's stay is [19] fastened to the head of the fore Mast by a strop [strap] and a dead man's eye [see below]. The maine top-gallant Mast's stay, in like manner, to the head of the fore top-Mast. The fore Masts and stayes belonging to them in like manner are fastened to the Boulspret and Spretsaile top-Mast, and those staies doe helpe to stay the Boulspret. The Misen staies doe come to the maine Mast, and the Misen top-Mast staies to the shrouds with Crowe's-feet. The use of

22

those staies are to keepe the Masts from falling aftwards,
or too much forwards.

Those *Lanniers* are many small Ropes reeved into the
dead men's eyes of all shrouds, either to slaken them or
set them taught; also all the staies have their blocks, and
dead men's eyes have *Lanniers*. *Dead men's eyes* are blocks,
some small, some great, with many holes but no shivers.
The *Crowe's-feet* reeved thorow them are a many of small
lines, sometimes 6, 8 or 10, but of small use more than
for fashion to make the Ship shew full of small Ropes.

Blocks or *Pullies* are thick peeces of wood having
Shivers [sheaves] in them, which is a little Wheele fixed
in the middest with a *Cocke* or *Pin*; some are Brasse, but
the most of Wood, whereon all the *running Ropes* doe
runne. Some are little, some great, with 3, 4, or 5 shivers
in them, and are called by the names of the Ropes whereto
they serve. There are also *double blocks*, that where there
is use of much strength, will purchase with much ease,
but not so fast as the other; and when wee hale [haul]
any Tackle or Haleyard to which two blocks doe belong,
when they meet, we call that *blocke and blocke*.[1]

The *Shrouds* are great Ropes which goe up either sides
of all Masts. The Misen, maine Mast and 1ore Mast
shrouds have at their lower ends dead men's eyes seased
into them, and are set up taught by Lanniers to the
Chaines. At the other end, over the heads of those Masts,
are pendants for *Tackels*, and *Swifters*[2] under them. The
top-Mast's shrouds in like manner are fastened with
Lanniers and dead men's eyes to the *Puttocks* [see below],
or plat[e]s of iron belonging to them, aloft over the head
of the Mast, as the other; and the *Chaines* are strong
plates[3] of iron fast bolted into the Ship's side by the [20]
Chaine waile.

A Lannier
[*lanyard*].

Dead men's eyes.

Crowe's-feet.

Blocks or Pullies
[*pulleys*].
Shivers.
A Cocke.
Running ropes.

Double blocks.

Block and block.

All Masts have
Shrouds, etc.

Chaines.

---

[1] The modern term is *double-blocked*, or *chock-a-block*.
[2] A rope from the masthead to the chain wales, for added strength.
[3] Or one long link, or several links of chain.

To Ease.
Taught [taut].

When the Shrouds are too stiffe, we say, *Ease them*; when too slacke, we say, *Set Taught the Shrouds*; but the Boulspret hath no Shrouds. And all those small ropes [that] doe crosse the Shrouds like steps are called *Ratlings*.

Ratlings
[Ratlines].
Puttocks [futtock shrouds].

The Puttocks[1] goe from the Shrouds of the fore Mast, maine Mast or misen, to goe off from the Shrouds into the *Top*, *Cap* or *Bowle*, which is a round thing at the head of either Mast for men to stand in; for when the Shrouds come neere the top of the Mast, they fall in so much that without the Puttocks you could not get into the Top, and in a manner they are a kinde of a Shroud.

Pendants
[pennants].

A *Pendant* is a short rope made fast at one end to the head of the Mast or the Yard's arme, having at the other end a blocke with a shiver to reeve some running rope in, as the Pendants of the backe staies and Tackles hang a little downe on the inside of the Shrouds. All Yards'-armes have them but the Misen, into which the Braces are reeved. And also there are Pendants or Streamers [that] hang from the yards' armes made of Taffaty [taffeta] or coloured flanell cloth, to beautifie the Ship onely.

Parrels.
Ribs.

Parrels are little round Balls called *Trucks*, and little peeces of wood called *ribs*, and ropes which doe incircle the Masts; and so made fast to the Yards that the Yards may slip up and downe easily upon the Masts, and with the helpe of the *Brest-rope*, doth keepe the Yard close to the Mast.

Bre[a]st-ropes.

Standing ropes.

The standing ropes are the shrouds and staies, because they are not removed [moved repeatedly], except it be to be eased or set taughter.

The Tackles are
of divers sorts,
etc.

The *Tackles* or ropes runne in three parts, having a Pendant with a blocke at the one end, and a blocke with a hooke at the other, to heave any thing in or out of the

---

[1] Synonymous with *futtocks*, in this case referring to the *futtock shrouds*.

The lower gun-deck of the Wasa, from the mainmast towards the stem. Above are the hatchway, carlings and ledges to which the deck planks are fastened (see page 8). Forward, the bits and crosspiece (see page 12). At right, the gun carriages, from which the cannon were removed shortly after the ship sank.

Console head. The Wasa's quarter galleries were supported by wooden console heads (brackets) carved as grotesque heads with wings (see page 13).

A model of a Swedish seaman dressed in clothes found in the Wasa.

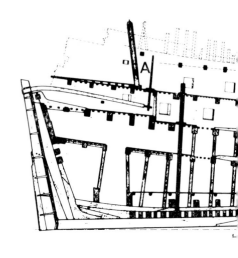

Below: Knees on the lower gun deck holding up the beams on the upper gundeck of the Wasa.

A reconstruction of the galley of the Wasa, *taken across the ship. Note that the kettle could move on a rolling axis, but not on a pitching axis.*

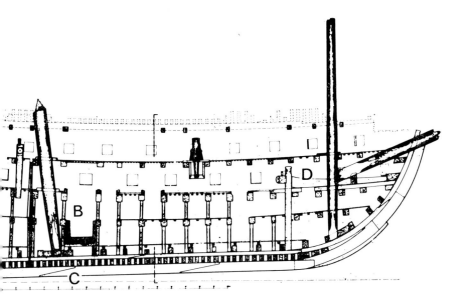

Profile plan of Wasa. *Note (A) the tiller and whipstaff arrangement aft, (B) galley, (C) the scarfed keel, and (D) the bits and their bracing.*

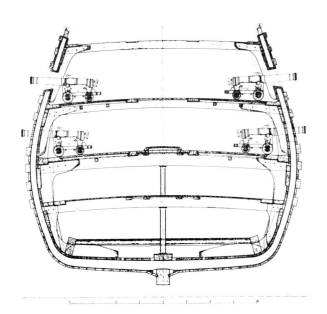

A cross-section of the Wasa.

The full scale reconstruction of the
Susan Constant, *lead ship of the
three which came to Virginia in
1607. The 100-ton vessel conforms
to all known specifications.*

A Traverse Board (see page 14).

ship. They are of divers sorts, as the *Bo[a]te's tackles*, made fast the one to the fore shrouds, the other to the maine, to hoise the Bote in or out; also the tackles that keepe firme the Masts from straying. The *Gunner's tackles* for haling in or out the Ordnances. But the *winding tackle* is the greatest, which is a great double blocke with three shivers, [fixed] to the end of a small Cable about the head of the Mast, and serveth as a [21] Pendant. To which is made fast to a *Guy*, which is a rope brought to it from the fore mast to keepe the weight upon it steady, or from swinging to and againe. Into the blocke is reeved a hawser, which is also reeved thorow another double blocke having in strop at the end of it, which put thorow the eye of the slings, is locked into it with a fid,[1] and so hoise the goods in or out by the helpe of the *Snap[snatch]-blocke*.[2]

 A Guy.

 Cat harpings are small ropes [which] runne in little blockes from one side of the ship to the other, neere the upper decke, to keepe the shrouds tight, for the more safety of the mast from rowling.

 Cat harpings.

 The *Halyards* belong to all masts for by them, we hoise the yards to their height; and the *Ties* are the ropes by which the yards doe hang, and doe carry up the yards when wee straine [at] the Halyards. The maine yard and fore yard ties are first reeved thorow the Ram's head [see p. 8], then thorow the Hounds [see p. 19], with a turne in the eye of the slings which are made fast to the yard. The misen yard and top yard have but single Ties, that is, one doth but run in one part; but the Spretsaile yard hath none, for it is made fast with a paire of slings to the boltspret.

 Halyards.
 The Ties.

 A *Horse* is a rope made fast to the fore mast shrouds and

 A Horse.

---

[1] A small marline-spike.

[2] Mainwaring, *op. cit.* II, 228. "A great block with the shiver in it, and a notch cut through one of the cheeks of it, by which notch they reeve any rope onto it."
This was quicker than having to reeve the rope through the sheaves.

the Spretsaile sheats, to keepe those sheats cleare of the anchor flookes.

To Sling.
Slings.

To sling is to make fast any caske, yard, ordnances or the like, in a paire of Slings; and *Slings* are made of a rope spliced at either end into it selfe, with one eye at either end, so long as to bee sufficient to receive the caske. The middle part of the rope also they seaze together, and so maketh another eye to hitch the hooke of the tackle. Another sort are made much longer for the hoising of ordnances; another is a chaine of iron to Sling or binde the yards fast aloft to the crosse trees in a fight, lest the ties should bee cut, and so the mast must fall.

Canhookes.

The *Canhookes* are two hookes fastened to the end of a rope with a noose, like this the Brewers use to sling or carry their barrels on, and those serve also to take in or out hogheads, or any other commodities.

A Parbunkell
(parbuckle].

A Parbunkel is two ropes that have at each end a noose or lumpe, that being [22] crossed, you may set any vessel, that hath but one head upon them, bringing but the loopes over the upper end of the caske, fix but the tackle to them, and then the vessell will stand strait in the middest, to heave out or take in without spilling.

Puddings.

Puddings are ropes nailed round to the yards' armes close to the end, a pretty distance one from another, to save the Robbins from galling upon the yards, or to serve [see p. 31] the anchor's ring to save the clinch[1] of the cable from galling. And the *Robbins* are little lines reeved into the eylet holes of the saile under the head ropes, to make fast the saile to the yard; for in stead of tying, sea men always say *Make fast. Head lines* are the ropes that make all the sailes fast to the yard.

Robbins
[robands].

Headlines.

Furling lines.

Furling lines are small lines made fast to the top saile, top gallant saile and the missen yards' armes. The missen

---

[1] Clinch: the knot by which the cable is fastened to the anchor ring.

hath but one, called the *smiting line*;[1] the other, on each   *A smiting line.*
side one, and by these we farthell[2] [furl], or binde up the
sailes. The *Brales* are small ropes reeved thorow Blockes   *Brales* [*brails*].
seased on each side [of] the ties, and come down before
the saile, and at the very skirt are fastened to the Creengles.   *Creengles*
With them we furle or farthell our sailes acrosse, and they   [*cringles*].
belong onely to the two courses and the missen. *To hale*
[haul] up the Brales, or *brale up the saile* is all one.
Creengles are little ropes spliced into the Bolt-ropes of all
sailes belonging to the maine and fore mast [some are
attached to the leech of the sail], to which the bolings
[bowline] bridles are made fast and [some to the bottom
of the sail] to hold by when we shake off a *Bonnet*. [See
p. 30.]

Boltropes is that rope [which] is sowed about every   *Bolt ropes.*
saile, soft and gently twisted, for the better s[t]owing and
handling the sailes. *Bunt lines* is but a small rope made   *Bunt lines.*
fast to the middest of the *Boltrope*, to a creengle reeved
thorow a small blocke which is seased to the yard, to trice
or draw up the Bunt of the saile when you farthell or
make it up.

The *Clew garnet* is a rope made fast to the clew of the   *Clew Garnet.*
saile, and from thence runnes in a blocke seased to the
middle of the yard, which in furling doth hale up the
clew of the saile close to the middle of the yard; and the
clew line is the same to the [23] top sailes, top gallant and   *Clew line.*
spret sailes, as the Clew garnet is to the maine and fore-
sailes. The *Clew* of a saile is the lowest corner next the
Sheat [sheet] and Tackes, and stretcheth somewhat
goaring or sloping from the square of the saile, and accord-   *Goaring*
   [*goring*].

---

[1] *Ibid*, II, 228. "A small rope which is made fast to the mizzen-
yard-arm below, next the deck; and when the mizzen-sail is farthelled
up, this is made alongst with it to the upper end of the yard (the
sail being made up with rope yarns), and so comes down by the
poop . . . ; . . . for when they pull this rope, that breaks all the rope
yarns, and so the sail comes down."

[2] From *furdel* ("to bundle") shortened to "furl."

ing to the Goaring, she is said to spread a *great* or a *little clew*.

Tackes [tacks].

Tackes are great ropes which, having a wall-knot at one end seased into the clew of the saile, and so reeved first thorow the chestres [chess trees],[1] and then commeth in at a hole in the ship's sides. This doth carry forward the clew of the saile to make it stand close by [to] a wind.

Sheats [sheets].

The *Sheats* are bent to the clews of all sailes. In the low sailes they hale aft the clew of the sailes, but in top sailes they serve to hale them home, that is, to bring the clew close to the yard's arme.

Braces.

The *Braces* belong to all yards but the missen. Every yard hath two reeved at their ends thorow two pendants, and those are to square the yards, or travasse [traverse] them as you please.

Boling [bowline].

The *Boling* is made fast to the leech of the saile about the middest, to make it stand the sharper or closer by a wind. It is fastened by two, three or foure ropes like a crow's foot, to as many parts of the saile, which is called

Boling bridles.

the *Boling bridles*, onely the missen Boling is fastened to the lower end of the yard. This rope belongs to all sailes except the Spret-saile and Spret-saile Top-saile, which not having any place to hale it forward by, they cannot

Sharp the Boling.
Checke the
Boling.

use those sailes by a wind [to windward]. *Sharp the maine Boling*, is to hall it taught. *Hale up the Boling*, is to pull it harder forward on. *Checke or ease the Boling*, is to let it be more slacke.

Lee fanng
[fange].
Reeving.

Lee fanngs[2] is a rope reeved into the creengles of the courses, when wee would hale in the bottome of the saile to lash on a bonnet or take in the saile; and *Reeving* is but drawing a rope thorow a blocke or oylet [eyelet] to runne up and down.

Leech lines.

Leech lines are small ropes made fast to the Leech of

---

[1] A timber bolted outboard of the ship, to which the sheets and tacks were hove down.

[2] A Vang is one of the two ropes that steadies the gaff or mizzen yard.

the top-sailes, for they belong to no other, and are reeved into a blocke at the yard, close by the top-saile ties, to hale in the Leech of the saile when you take them in. The *Leech* of a saile is the outward side of a skirt of a saile, from the earing to the clew; and the *Earing* is that part of the bunt rope [sic. boltrope p. 27] [24] which at all the foure corners of the saile is left open, as it were a ring. The two upmost parts are put over the ends of the yards' armes, and so made fast to the yards, and the lowermost are seased or *Bent* to the sheats, and tackes into the clew.[1]

The *Lifts* are two ropes which belong to all yards' armes, to *top the yards*, that is, to make them hang higher or lower at your pleasure. But the top-saile Lifts doe serve for sheats to the top gallant yards; the haling them is called the *Topping the Lifts*, as *Top a starboard*, or *Top a port*.

Legs are small ropes put thorow the bolt ropes of the maine and fore saile, neere to a foot in length, spliced each end into the other in the leech of the saile, having a little eye whereunto the *Martnets* are fastened by two hitches, and the end seased into the standing parts of the Martnets; which are also small lines like crow feet, reeved thorow a blocke at the top mast head, and so comes downe by the mast to the decke; but the top-saile martnets are made fast to the head of the top gallant mast, and commeth but to the top, where it is haled, and called the *Top Martnets*.[2] They serve to bring that part of the leech next the yards' arme up close to the yard "when we farthell the saile" H.M.

Latchets are small lines sewed in the Bonnets and Drablers[3] [see p. 30], like loops, to lash or make fast the Bonnet to the course, or the course [sic; bonnet] to the

Leech of a saile.
Earings.

Bent.
Lifts.

Topping the Lifts.

Legs.

Mart[i]net.

Latchets.

---

[1] *Ibid.*, II, 143 [*sic*], ". . . to the lowermost, the tacks and sheets are seized, or (as the more proper term is), they are bent unto the clew."

[2] *Ibid.*, II, 185 [*sic*], "the term is *Top the Martinets*."

[3] OED gives this as "drabbler," but most references give it as "drabler."

Lashing.

Drabler, which we call *Lashing the Bonnet to the course,* or *the Drabler to the Bonnet.*

The Loofe [*luff*] *hook.*

The *Loofe hooke* is a tackle with two hookes; one to hitch into a chingle [sic; cringle] of the maine or fore saile, in the bolt-rope in the leech of the saile by the clew; and the other to a strap spliced to the chestres [chess trees]

Bouse.
A Bonnet.
A Drabler.
A Course.

to *bouse* or pull downe the saile to succour the tackes in a stiffe gale of wind, or take off or put on a *Bonnet* or a *Drabler,* which are two short sailes to take off or put to the *forecourse* or the *maine* [course], which is the fore saile or maine saile.

A Knave line.

The *Knave-line* is a rope [which] hath one end fastened to the crosse trees, and so comes downe by the ties to the Ram's head, to which is seased a small peece of wood some two foot long with a hole in the end, whereunto the line is reeved and brought to the ship's side, and haled taught to the [25] Railes to keepe the ties and Halyards from turning about one another when they are new.

Knettels [*knittles*].

Knettels are two rope yarnes twisted together, and a knot at each end, whereunto to sease a blocke, a rope, or

Rope yarnes.

the like. *Rope yarnes* are the yarnes of any rope untwisted. They serve to sarve [serve; see p. 31] small ropes, or make Sinnet, Mats, Plats, or Caburnes, and make up the sailes

Sinnet [*sennet*].

at the yards' armes. *Sinnet* is a string made of rope yarne, commonly of two, foure, six, eight or nine strings, platted in three parts; which being beat flat, they use it to sarve

Mats or Panch.

ropes or *Mats.* That which we call a *Panch* are broad-clouts,[1] woven of *Thrums*[2] and Sinnet together, to save things from galling about the maine and fore yards at the ties, and also from the masts; and upon the Boltspret, Loufe, Beakehead or Gunwaile, to save the clewes of the sailes from galling or fretting.

Caburne.

Caburne is a small line make of spun yarne, to make a

---

[1] This rare word could not be found, although its synonym is *panch.*

[2] Mats made by passing small tufts of rope yarn through canvas, like a string rug.

bend of two Cables, or to sease the Tackels, or the like.
Seasing is to binde fast any ropes together with some small
rope yarne. Marline[1] is any line to a blocke, or any tackell,
Pendant, Garnet, or the like. There is also a rope by
which the Boat doth ride by the ship's side, which we cal
a *Seasen.* To *sarve* any rope with plats or Sinnet is but
to lay Sinnet, Spun yarne, Rope yarne, or a peece of
Canvas upon the rope, and then rowle it fast to keepe the
rope from galling about the shrowds at the head of the
masts, the Cable in the Hawse, the flooke of the Anchor,
the Boat rope, or any thing. *Spunyarne* is nothing but
rope yarne made small at the ends, and so spun one to
another so long as you will with a winch. Also *Caskets*
are but small ropes of Sinnet made fast to the gromits or
rings upon the yards; the longest are in the midst of the
yards betwixt the ties, and are called the bre[a]st Caskets,
hanging on each side the yard in small lengths, only to
binde up the saile when it is furled.

Marling is a small line of untwisted hemp, very pliant
and well tarred, to sease the ends of Ropes from ravel[l]ing
out, or the sides of the blockes at their arses;[2] or if the
saile rent out of the Bolt-rope, they will make it fast with
marlin [26] till they have leisure to mend it. The *marling
spike* is but a small peece of iron to splice ropes together,
or open the bolt rope when you sew the saile. *Splicing* is
so to let one rope's end into another, [that] they shall be
as firme as if they were but one rope, and this is called a
round Splice; the *cut Splice*[3] is to let one into another with
as much distance as you will, and yet bee strong, and undoe
when you will.

Now to make an end of this discourse with a *knot*, you
are to know Sea-men use three. The first is called the

Seasing [seizing].

*seasen
[seizing].
Sarve [serve] or
Sirvis [service].*

Spunyarne.

Caskets [gaskets].

*Marling
[marline].*

Marling spike.

Splicing.

*A round Splice.
A cut Splice.*

A Knot.

---

[1] This appears to be an error; see *marling* (marline) below.
[2] The breech-end, or bottom of a block.
[3] Mainwaring, *op. cit.*, II, 231: Cunt-splice.

A Wall [wale] knot.

A Boling [bowline] knot.

Sheepshanks Knot.

Wall knot, which is a round knob, so made with the strounds [strands] or layes of a rope, [that] it cannot slip; the Sheates, Ta[c]kes and Stoppers[1] use this knot. The *Boling knot* is also so firmly made and fastened by the bridles into the creengles of the sailes, they will breake or the saile split before it will slip.

The last is the *She[e]pshanke*, which is a knot they cast upon a Runner or Tackle when it is too long, to take in the goods; and by this knot they can shorten a rope without cutting it, as much as they list, and presently undoe it againe, and yet never the worse.

[1] Stoppers: a short length of rope or chain, for checking the running of a rope or chain, or holding it firmly while it is being belayed.

Chapter VI

What doth belong to the Boats and Skiffe, with the definition of all those thirteene Ropes which are onely properly called Ropes belonging to a Ship and the Boat and their use.

Of Boats there are divers sorts, but those belonging to ships are called either the *long Boat* or *Ship's Boat*, which should bee able to weigh her sheat anchor. Those will live in any reasonable sea, especially the long Boat. Great ships have also other small Boats called *Shallops* and *Skiffes*, which are [with] more [27] ease and lesse trouble rowed to and againe upon any small occasion.

To a Boat belongs a mast and saile, a stay, sheat & Halyard, Rudder & Rudder irons, as to a ship. Also in any discovery [exploration] they use a *Tarpawling*, which is a good peece of Canvas washed over with Tar, to cover the *Bailes* or hoopes over the sterne of their Boat where they lodge in an harbor, which is that you call a Tilt[1] covered with wadmall[2] in your *Wherries*;[3] or else an *Awning*, which is but the bot[e]s saile or some peece of an old saile brought over the yard and stay, and boumed out with the boat hooke, so spread over their heads; which is also much used as well a shore as in a ship, especially in hot countreys, to keepe men from the extremity of heat or wet, which is very oft infectious.

A long Boat.

A Shallop.
A Skiffe.

Tarpawling
[tarpaulin].
Bailes [Bales].

Awning.

[1] An awning.
[2] Thick, coarse woollen cloth used for rough purposes.
[3] A type of river rowing boat.

Thoughts
[*thwarts*].
Thowles
[*thole pins*].

Thoughts are the seats whereon the Rowers sit; and *Thowles*, small pins put into little holes in the Gunwaile or upon the Boat's side, against which they beare the oares when they row. They have also a Daved [davit], and also in long Boats a windlesse to weigh the anchor by, which is with more ease than the ship can.

A Gang.

The two arching timbers against the Boat head are called *Carlings*. *Man the Boat* is to put a *Gang* of men, which is a company, into her. They are commonly called the *Coxswaine's Gang*, who hath the charge of her. *Free the Boat* is to baile or cast out the water. *Trim the Boat* is to keepe her str[a]ight. *Winde the Boat* is to bring her head the other way. *Hold water* is to stay her. *Forbeare* is to hold still any oare you are commanded, or on the broad or whole side. *A fresh Spell* is to releeve the Rowers with another Gang. *Give the Boat more way for a dram of the bottell, who saies Amends,*[1] *one and all, Vea, vea, vea, yea, yea!* That is, they pull all strongly together.

Free or Baile.
Trim Boat.
Winde Boat.
Hold water.
Forbeare.
A Spell.

Vea, vea, vea.

The Entering rope.
Bucket rope.

The *Entering rope* is tied by the ship's side, to hold by as you goe up the Entering ladder, cleats, or wailes.

The *Bucket rope*, that is tied to the Bucket, by which you hale and draw water up by the ship's side.

Bolt ropes.
Port ropes.
Jeare rope.

The *Bolt ropes* are those wherein the sailes are sowed.

The *Port ropes* hale up the Ports of the Ordnances.

The *Jeare rope* is a peece of a hawser made fast to the [28] maine yard, another to the fore yard close to the ties, reeved thorow a blocke which is seased close to the top, and so comes downe by the mast, and is reeved thorow another blocke at the bottome of the mast close by the decke. Great ships have on each side the ties one, but small ships none. The use is to helpe to hoise up the yard to succour the ties, which though they breake, yet they would hold up the mast.

[1] In the *Accidence*, this is given as *amen*. However, these may be variations of *amaine*, which, as one of its definitions, meant *surrender*, or *give in* (see p. 77). *Amaine* also meant *all at once*.

34

The *Preventer rope* is a little one seased crosse over the ties, that if one part of them should breake, yet the other should not runne thorow the Ram's head to indanger the yard.

Preventer rope.

The *Top ropes* are those wherewith we set or strike the maine or fore Top masts. It is reeved thorow a great blocke seased under the Cap, reeved thorow the heele of the Top mast thwart ships, and then made fast to a ring with a clinch on the other side the Cap. The other part comes downe by the ties, reeved into the Knights, and so brought to the Capstaine when they set the Top masts.

Tope ropes.

The Keele rope, you have read in the [chapter on] building, is of haire, in the Keele, to scower the Limber holes.

Keele ropes.

The *Rudder rope* is reeved thorow the stern post, and goeth thorow the head of the Rudder, and then both ends spliced together serves to save the Rudder if it should bee strucke off the irons.

Rudder rope.

The *Cat rope* is to hale up the Cat.

Cat rope.

The *Boy rope* is that which is tied to the b[u]oy by the one end, and the anchor's flooke by the other.[1]

B[u]oy rope.

The *Boat rope* is that which the ship doth tow her Boat by, at her sterne.

Boat rope.

The *Ghest rope* is added to the Boat rope when shee is towed at the ship's sterne, to keepe her from *shearing*, that is, from swinging to and againe; for in a stiffe gale she will make such yawes,[2] and have such girds,[3] it would indanger her to bee torne in peeces, but that they use to *swift* her, that is, to incircle the Gunwaile with a good rope, and to that make fast the Ghest rope. [29]

Ghest [guest] rope.
Shearing.

Swifting.

---

[1] By this means, the anchor could be located or raised.
[2] Yaw: to deviate momentarily from the intended course.
[3] Girts: the boat swinging against the taut boat rope.

Chapter VII

The names of all sorts of Anchors, Cables and Sailes, and how they beare their proportions, with their use. Also how the Ordnances should bee placed, and the goods stowed in a ship.

A Kedger [Kedge].

The proper tearmes belonging to Anchors are many. The least [smallest] are called *Kedgers*, to use in calme weather in a slow streame, or to kedge up and downe a narrow River, which is when they feare the winde or tide may drive them on shore. They row by her with an Anchor in a boat, and in the middest of the streame or where they finde most fit, [drop anchor] if the Ship come too neere the shore, and so by a Hawser winde her head about, then waigh it againe till the like occasion; and this is *kedging*.

Streame Anchor.
The first.
Second.
Third Anchor.
Sheat [sheet] Anchor.

There is also a *streame Anchor*, not much bigger, to stemme an easie stream or tide.[1] Then there is the *first*, *second* and *third Anchor*, yet all such as a Ship in faire weather may ride by, and are called *Bow Anchors*.

The greatest is the *sheat Anchor*, and never used but in great necessity.

An Anchor's shanke.
Flook [fluke].
Shoulder.

They are commonly made according to the burthen of the Ship by proportion, for that the sheat Anchor of a small ship will not serve for a Kedger to a great ship. Also it beareth a proportion in it selfe, as the one *flooke*, which is that [part which] doth sticke in the ground, is but the third part of the *shanke* in length. At the head of

[1] To hold the ship fast whilst the tide runs against it.

the Shanke there is a hole called an *Eye*, and in it a *Ring*,   *Beame or Nut.*[1]
wherein is the *Nut*, to which there is fast fixed a *Stocke*   *Eye.*
of wood crossing the Flookes, and the length is taken from   *Ring.*
the length of the Shanke. These [30] differ not in shape   *Stocke.*
but in waight, from two hundred to three or foure
thousand waight. *Grapells* or *Graplings* [grapnels] are the
least of all, and have foure flookes (but no stock), for a
boat to ride by, or to throw into a ship in a fight, to pull
downe the gratings or hold fast.

The *Cables* also carry a proportion to the Anchors, but   *A Cable, the*
if it be not three strond, it is accounted but a Hawser.   *first, second and*
Yet a great ship's Hawser may be a Cable to the sheat   *third.*
Anchor for a small ship; and there is the *first*, *second*, and
third Cable, besided the *Sheat Anchor Cable*. If the Cable   *Sheat Anchor*
bee well made, we say it is *well laid*. To *Keckell or sarve*   *Cable.*
the Cable, as is said, is but to bind some old clouts to keepe *Keckell [Keckle].*
it from galling in the Hawse or Ring. [To] *Splice a*   *Splice.*
Cable, is to fasten two ends together, that is may be double
in length, to make the Ship ride with more ease, and is
called a *shot of Cable*. [To] *Quoile a Cable* is to lay it up   *A Shot of Cable.*
in a round Ring or *Fake*, one above another. *Pay more*   *Quoile [coil].*
Cable, is when you carry an Anchor [and cable] out in   *A Fake.*
the boat, to turne over [into the sea some cable, that the   *Pay.*
boat may tow easier and the cable be slack. H. W.].
Pay cheap is when you overset it,[2] or turnes it over board   *Pay cheape.*
faster [fling it over apace. H. W.]. *Veere more Cable* is
when you ride at Anchor [to let more go out]. And *end*   *End for end.*
for end is when the Cable runneth cleare out of the
Hawse, or any Rope out of his shiver.

---

[1] *Sic.* Here Smith or the printer were badly in error. *Beame* and
Shanke are synonymous: the nut was the ball at the upper end of the
shank and the eye was in the nut.

[2] The word *overset* is misleading, since its ordinary meaning was
capsize; but in this case (*ibid.*, II, 194): "the turning over [board] of
any cable or small rope which is coiled up."

A Bight.
A Bitter.

A Bitter's end.
Gert [girt].

To Bend.
Unbend.

Bending.

Hitch.

Fenders.
Junkes.

Bre[a]stfast.

Sternfast.

Rousing.
Shank-pa[i]nter.

Stop.

Boyes [buoys].

Can Boyes.

A *Bight* is to hold by any part of a coile, that is, the upmost fake. A *Bitter* is but the turne of a Cable about the Bits, and veare it out by little and little. And the *Bitter's end* is that part of the Cable [that] doth stay within boord. *Gert*, is when the Cable is so taught, that upon the turning of a tide, a Ship cannot goe over it.

To bend the Cable to the Anchor is to make it fast to the Ring; [to] *unbend* the Cable is but to take it away, which we usually doe when we are at Sea; and to tie two ropes or Cables together is called *bending*. *Hitch*, is to catch hold of any thing with a rope to hold it fast, or with a hooke, as, *hitch the fish-hooke to the Anchor's flooke*, or *the Tackles into the Garnets of the Slings*.

Fenders are peeces of old Hawsers called *Junkes*, hung over the ship sides to keepe them from brusing. In boats they use poles or boat-hooks to fend off the boat from brusing.

A *Brest-fast* is a [31] rope which is fastened to some part of the Ship forward on, to hold her head to a wharfe or any thing; and a *Sterne-fast* is the same in the Sterne. The use for the Hawser is to warp the Ship by, which is laying out an Anchor, and winde[ing] her up to it by a Capsterne. *Rousing* is but pulling the slacknesse of any Cables with men's hands into the Ship. The *Shank-painter* is a short chaine fastend under the fore mast's shrouds with a bolt to the ship's sides, and at the other end a rope to make fast the Anchor to the Bow [mostly in a harbour or road].

To stop is when you come to an Anchor, and veares out your Cable, but by degrees, till the Ship ride well, then they say, *Stop the Ship*. To those Cables and Anchors belongs short peeces of wood called *Boyes*, or close hooped barrels like Tankards, as is said, but much shorter, to show you the Anchor and helpe to waigh it. There is another sort of Cans called *Can Boyes*, much greater, mo[o]red upon shoules to give Marriners warning of the dangers.

38

The *maine saile* and the *fore saile* is called the *fore course* and the *maine course*, or a *paire of courses*. Bonits and *Drablers* are commonly one third part a peece to the saile they belong unto in depth, but their proportion is uncertaine; for some will make the maine saile so deepe that with a shallow bonet they will cloath all the Mast without a Drabler; but without bonets we call them but courses. We say, *Lash on the bonet to the course*, because it is made fast with Latchets into the eylot holes of the saile, as the Drabler is to it, and used as the wind permits. There is also your *maine top-saile*, and *fore top-saile*, with their *top-gallant sailes*, and in a faire gaile your *studding sailes*, which are bolts of Canvasse or any cloth that will hold wind, [which] wee extend alongst the side of the maine saile, and boomes it out with a boome or long pole; which we use also sometimes to the clew of the maine saile, fore saile and spret saile when you goe before the wind, or quartering, else not.

Your *Miszen* and *Miszen top-saile*, your *Spret* and *Spret top-saile*, as the rest, take all their names of their yards.

A *Drift saile* is onely used under water, veared out right a head by sheats, [32] to keepe the Ship's head right upon the Sea in a storme, or when a ship drives too fast in a current. A *Netting saile* is onely a saile laid over the *Netting*, which is small ropes from the top of the fore castle to the Poope[1], stretched upon the ledges from the *Waist-trees* [see p. 11] to the *Roufe-trees*; which are onely small Timbers to beare up the Gratings from the halfe Decke to the fore-castle, supported by *Stantions* that rest upon the halfe Decke; and this Netting, or *Grating*, which is but the like made of wood, you may set up or take downe when you please, and is called the *close fights*, fore and aft.

Sailes.
Maine Saile.
Fore Saile.
Maine course.
Fore course.
Bonits [bonnets].
Drablers.

Maine top Saile.
Fore top Saile.
Top gallant Sailes.
Studding Sailes.

Misen.
Misen top Saile.
Spret saile.
Spretsaile top-saile.
Drift Saile.
Netting Saile.
Nettings.

Waist-trees.
Roufe-trees.
Stantions [stanchions].
Gratings.

---

[1] The upmost part of the aft end of the vessel which usually was the roof of the Master's cabin.

Head Sailes.

Now the use of those sailes is thus: all *head Sailes*, which are those belonging to the fore Mast and Boltspret, doe keepe the Ship from the wind, or cause her to fall off.

After Sailes.

All *after sailes*, that is, all the sailes belonging to the maine Mast and Miszen, keepes her to wind ward; therefore few ships will steare upon quarter winds with one saile, but must have one after saile and one head saile. The sailes are cut in proportion, as the Masts and Yards are, in bredth and length; but the Spret-saile is 3/4 parts the depth of the fore saile, and the Miszen, by the Leech, twise so deepe as the Mast is long from the Decke to the Hounds. The

Leech.

Leech of a saile is the outward side or skirt of the saile from the earing to the clew, the middle betwixt which

The Clew.

wee account the Leech. The *Clew* is the lower corner of a Saile, to which you make fast your Sheates and Tacks,

Goring.

or that part which comes *goring* out from the square of the saile, for a square saile hath no Clew;[1] but the mainesaile must bee cut goring, because the Tacks will come closer aboord, and so cause the saile to hold more wind. Now when the Saile is large and hath a good Clew, we say *She spreds a large Clew*, or *spreds much Canvas*.

In making those sailes they use two sorts of seames downe the Sailes, which doth sow the bredth of the

A Monke [monkey] seame.
A Round seame.

Canvas together; the one we call a *Munk seame*, which is flat, the other a *round seame*, which is so called because it is round.

The Ship being thus provided, there wants yet her Ordnances, which should be in greatnesse according to her [33] building, in strength and burthen; but the greatest

A Tier.
Second.
Third.

commonly lieth lowest, which we call the *lower tier*, if she bee furnished fore and aft. Likewise the *second Tier*, and the *third*, which are the smallest. The fore-Castle and the halfe Decke being also furnished, wee account

Halfe a Tier.

halfe a Tier.

---

[1] On a modern fore-and-aft rigged sailing craft, the clew of the sail is that corner which is attached to the aft end of the boom.

Stowage or *to stow*,[1] is to put the goods in [the] Howle in order, the most ponderous next the Ballast, which is next the Keelson, to keepe her stiffe[2] in the Sea. *Ballast* is either Gravell, Stones or Lead, but that which is driest, heaviest, and lies closest is best. To finde a leake, they *trench the Ballast*, that is, to divide it. The Ballast wil sometimes *shoot*, that is, run from one side to another, and so will Corne and Salt if you make not Pouches or Bulk-heads, which when the Ship doth heeld [heel], is very dangerous to overset or turne the Keele upwards. For Caske, that is so stowed tier above tier with Ballast, and *Canting Coines*, which are little short peeces of wood or Billets cut with a sharpe ridge or edge, to lye betwixt the Caske; and *standing Coines* are Billets or Pipe-staves,[3] to make them [so] they cannot give way nor stirre.

The Ship will *beare* much, that is, carry much Ordnance or goods, or beare much saile; and when you let any thing downe into the Howle, lowering it by degrees, [if they would have it come down as fast as it can. H. M.] they say, *Amaine!* and being downe, *Strike!*[4] [34]

Stowage.
To Stow.
Ballast.

Trench the Ballast.
Shout. [*Shoot*]

Canting Coines.
[*Cantic quoins*].
Standing Coines.

To beare.

---

[1] It also means to confine men below the hatches; also to furl sail.

[2] *Stiff*: the power or ability of a vessel to offer resistance to inclination from the upright, caused by external forces, as the wind, or a rough sea; the opposite of *crank* or *walt*.

[3] Large barrel staves.

[4] However, *to strike amaine* meant to let fall the top sails as a sign of surrender.

Chapter VIII

The charge and duty of the Captaine of a ship, and every Office and Officer in a man of Warre'[1].

The Captaine's charge.

The *Captaine's charge* is to command all, and tell the Master to what Port hee will goe, or to what Height [latitude]. In a fight he is to give direction for the managing thereof, and the Master is to see the cunning[2] of the ship, and trimming of the sailes.

The Master and his Mates.

The *Master* and his *Mates* are to direct the course, command all the Sailers for stearing, trimming and sailing the ship. His Mates are only his seconds, allowed sometimes for the two mid ships men, that ought to take charge of the first prize [captured ship].

The Pilot.

The *Pilot*, when they make land, doth take the charge of the ship till he bring her to harbour.

The Chirurgion [surgeon] and his Mate.

The *Chirurgion* is to be exempted from all duty but to attend the sicke and cure the wounded; and good care would be had he have a certificate from Barber Chirurgions' Hall[3] of his sufficiency, and also that his chest be well furnished both for Physicke [medicine] and Chirurgery [surgery], and so neare as may be proper for that clime you goe for, which neglect hath beene the losse of many a man's life.

The Cape-merchant or Purser.

The *Cape-merchant* or *Purser* hath the charge of all the

---

[1] This section is not based on Mainwaring.

[2] *Conning*: to give orders to the helmsman.

[3] The Company of Barber Surgeons was incorporated in 1461. Under Henry VIII it was changed to the Company of Barbers and Surgeons, and only barbers were allowed to practise dentistry.

Carragasoune[1] or merchandize, and doth keepe an account of all that is received or delivered; but a man of Warre hath onely a Purser.

The *Master Gunner* hath the charge of the ordnance and shot, powder, match, ladles, spunges, wormes, cartrages, [35] armes and fire-workes [see p. 87]; and the rest of the *Gunners* or *quarter Gunners* to receive their charge from him according to directions, and to give an account of their store.

The Gunner with his Mate, and quarter Gunners.

The *Carpenter* and his *Mate* is to have the nailes, clinches,[2] roove [rove] and clinch nailes,[3] spikes, plates, rudder irons, pumpe nailes,[4] skupper nailes[5] and leather, sawes, files, hatchets and such like, and ever ready for calking, breaming, stopping leakes, fishing or splicing the masts or yards [see p. 21] as occasion requireth, and to give an account of his store.

The Carpenter and his Mate.

The *Boatswaine* is to have the charge of all the cordage, tackling, sailes, fids and marling spikes, needles, twine, saile-cloth, and rigging the ship; his *Mate*, the command of the long boat for the setting forth of anchors, weighing or fetching home an anchor,[6] warping, towing or moring; and to give an account of his store.

The Boatswaine and his Mate.

The *Trumpeter* is always to attend the Captaine's command, and to sound either at his going a shore or comming aboord; at the entertainment of strangers; also when you hale a ship, when you charge, boord or enter; and the poope is his place to stand or sit upon. If there bee a noise, they are to attend him; if there be not, every one hee doth teach to beare a part. The Captaine is to

The Trumpeter.

---

[1] *Caragazon*: bill of lading, in Spanish. This was altered to cargo, and the meaning altered to its present usage.

[2] Nails or bolts which are driven through, and have their ends burred.

[3] The same, but the ends are burred over a washer, called a *rove*.

[4], [5] Large-headed tacks used to nail leather to pumps, scuppers, or elsewhere.

[6] It was sometimes easier to weigh anchor and bring it back to the ship with the longboat than by the ship's capstan.

incourage him by increasing his shares or pay, and give the Master Trumpeter a reward.

The Marshall.

The *Marshall* is to punish offenders and to see justice executed according to directions; as ducking at the yard's arme,[1] ha[u]ling under the keele, bound to the capsterne or maine mast with a basket of shot about his necke, setting in the *bilbowes*,[2] and *to pay the Cobtie*,[3] or *the Morioune*.[4] But the boyes the Boatswaine is to see every Munday at the chest to say their compasse,[5] and receive their punishment for all their weeke's offences; which done, they are to have a quarter can of beare and a basket of bread. But if the Boatswaine eat or drinke before hee catch them, they are free.

The Corporall.

The *Corporall* is to see [to] the setting and releeving the watch, and see all the souldiers and sailers keepe their armes [36] cleane, neat and yare [smart], and teach them their use.

The Steward and his Mate.

The *Steward* is to deliver out the victuals according to the Captaine's directions, and messe them foure, five or six, as there is occasion.

The quarter Masters.

The *quarter Masters* have the charge of the howle for stowing, romaging [rummaging],[6] and trimming the ship in the hold, and of their squadrons for the watch; and for fishing, to have a Sayne [seine], a fisgig [fishing spear], a harpin iron [harpoon], and fish hooks for *Porgos* [porgies], *Bonetos, Dolphins* or *Dorados,* and rayling lines [drop lines] for *Mackrels.*

---

[1] Suspended by a rope reeved through a block on the end of a yard-arm, and repeatedly ducked in the water.

[2] *Bilboes*: long iron bars with sliding shackles that held the ankles.

[3] *Cobbing*: to beat with a barrel-stave, preferably with that stave containing the bung-hole, for the decorative effect.

[4] *Morion*: a military punishment, in which the miscreant was beaten with a pikestaff.

[5] To box the compass, or recite the 32 major compass points.

[6] Arranging or rearranging cargo; also defined as having the bilges cleaned.

The *Cooper* is to looke to the caske, hoopes and twigs,[1] to stave or repaire the buckets, baricos,[2] cans,[3] steepe-tubs, runlets,[4] hogsheads [63 gals.], pipes [126 gals.], but[t]s,[5] etc. for wine, beare, sider, beverage, fresh water, or any liquor.

The Cooper aud his mate.

The *Coxswaine* is to have a choise Gang to attend the skiffe, to goe to and againe as occasion commandeth.

The Coxswaine and his Mate.

The *Cooke* is to dresse and deliver out the victual. He hath his store of quarter cans, small cans, platters, spoones, lanthornes [lanterns], etc., and is to give his account of the remainder.

The Cooke and his Mate.

The *Swabber* is to wash and keepe cleane the ship and maps [mops].

The Swabber.

The *Liar* is to hold his place but for a weeke, and hee that is first taken with a lie, every Munday is so proclaimed at the maine mast by a generall cry, *A Liar, a Liar, a Liar.* Hee is under the Swabber, and onely to keepe cleane the beake head and chaines.[6]

The Lyar [liar].

The Sailers are the ancient men,[7] for hoising the sailes, getting the tacks aboord, haling the bowlings, and stearing the ship.

The Sailers.

The *Younkers* are the young men called *Fore-mast men*, to take in the top-sailes, or top and yard,[8] for furling the sailes, or slinging the yards, bousing or trising, and take their turnes at helme.

The Younkers [youngsters].

[1] Supple, long, split saplings used as barrel hoops.
[2] An oval cask, so made to prevent it rolling about at sea.
[3] A can was a container of tin or other metal, larger than a drinking vessel, with a handle on top, like a bucket.
[4] A small cask for cordials or distilled liquors, as brandy, from one pint to eighteen and a half gals. capacity.
[5] A cask for beer or ale, from 108–140 gallons, depending on the liquid it contained. It was generally equal to a pipe, or 126 gals. Two pipes were equal in capacity to a tun.
[6] Both these places were used as latrines.
[7] Obs. term for *Ensign*, but here it seems to mean the experienced men.
[8] I believe this an error for *top a yard*, which meant to raise one end of the yard higher than the other, or *top the yard*, which meant to level the yard.

The Lieutenant his place.

The *Lieutenant* is to associate [with] the Captaine, and in his absence to execute his place. Hee is to see the Marshall and Corporall doe their duties, and assist them in instructing [37] the souldiers; and in a fight the forecastle is his place to make good, as the Captaine doth the halfe decke, and the Quarter Master's or Master's Mate the midships; and in a States [Netherlands] man of Warre,¹ he is allowed as necessary as a Lieutenant on shore.

¹ In Smith's time, Holland was known as the Republic of the Seven United Provinces. The representative governing body was called the States General, hence the term "A States' Man-of-war."

Chapter IX

Proper Sea tearmes for dividing the company at Sea, and stearing, sayling, or moring a Ship in faire weather, or in a storme.

It is to bee supposed by this [time] the Ship is victualled and manned, the voiage determined; the *steepe Tubs* in the chains to shift their Beefe,[1] Porke or Fish in salt water till the salt be out (though not the saltnesse), and all things else ready to set saile.

But before wee goe any further, for the better understanding the rest, a few words for *stearing* and *cunning* the Ship would not bee amisse.

Then know, *Star-boord* is the right hand, *Lar-boord* the left. *Starboord the Helme* is to put the Helme a Starboord, then the ship will goe to the Larboord. *Right your Helme*, that is to keepe it in the *mid ships*, or right up. *Port*, that is to put the Helme to Larboord, and the Ship will goe to the Starboord; for the Ship will ever goe contrary to the Helme.

Now by a quarter wind they will say *Aloofe*, or *Keepe your Loofe, keepe her to it, have a care of your Lee-Latch.*[2] *Touch the wind* and *warre no more*[3] is no more but to bid him at the Helme to keepe her so neere the wind as may

Steep Tubs.

Stearing.
Cunning [conning].
Starboord [starboard].
Larboord [larboard].
Mid-ships.
Port.
A loofe [a'luff].
Keep your loofe.
War [veer] no more.

[1] To change the water in which something is being steeped or soaked, or to transfer it to other water.

[2] *Ibid.*, II, 178: "to look that the ship go not to the leeward of her course."

[3] There is some question whether this meant *Beware, no more*, or, *veer*, or *wear no more*.

47

No neare.
Ease.
Steady.
Yare.

be. *No neere, ease the Helme!* or *Beare up!*, is to let her fall to Lee-ward. *Steady*, that is to keepe [38] her right upon that point your steare by. *Be yare*[1] *at the Helme!*, or, *A fresh man to the Helme!* But he that keepes the Ship most from yawing doth commonly use the le[a]st motion with the Helme, and those steare the best.

The Master and company being aboord, he commands them to *Get the sailes to the yards, and about your geare*,

Geare.

or, *Worke on all hands, stretch forward your maine*

Predy.

Halliards, hoise your Sailes halfe mast high. Predy!, or, *Make ready to set saile. Crosse your yards,*[2] *bring your Cable to the Capsterne. Boatswaine, fetch an Anchor aboord. Breake ground*, or, *Weigh Anchor! Heave a head! Men*

A Pike [a'peak].

into the Tops! Men upon the yards! Come, is the Anchor a' pike? That is, to heave the Hawse of the ship right over the Anchor. *What, is the Anchor away?*

Yea, yea!

Tally.

Let fall your fore-saile. Tally! That is, hale off the Sheats. *Who is at the Helme there? Coile your Cables in small fakes! Hale the Cat!*[3] *A Bitter, . . . belay, . . . loose fast your Anchor with your shank-painter! Stow the Boat!*

Set the land, how it beares by the Compasse, that we may the better know thereby to keep our account and direct our course.

Let fall your maine saile, every man say his private prayer for a boone [bon] *voyage! Out with your spret saile, on with your bonits & Drablers, steare steady & keep your course, so you go wel!*

How they divide the company at sea, and set, and rule the watch.

When this is done, the Captaine or Master commands the Boatswaine to call up the company. The Master, being chiefe of the Starboord watch, doth call one, and his right hand Mate on the Larboord doth call another,

---

[1] Quick, or smart.   [2] To hoist the yards to the mast-heads.
[3] To haul the anchor to the cat-head by the cat-rope.

and so forward, till they be divided in two parts. Then each man is to chuse his Mate, Consort, or Comrade, and then devide them into squadrons according to your number and burthen of your ship as you see occasion. These are to take their turnes at the Helme, trim sailes, pumpe, and doe all duties each halfe, or each squadron for eight Glasses or foure houres, which is a watch.

But care would bee had that there be not two Comrades upon one watch, because they may have the more roome in their Cabbins to rest. And as the Captaine and master's Mates, Gunners, Carpenters, Quartermasters, Trumpeters, etc. are to be abaft the Mast, so the [39] Boatswaine and all the Yonkers or common Sailers under his command is to be before the Mast.

The next is, to messe them foure to a messe, and then give every messe a quarter Can of beere and a basket of bread to stay their stomacks till the Kettle be boiled, that they may first goe to prayer, then to supper; and at six a'clocke sing a Psalme, say a Prayer, and the Master with his side begins the watch. Then all the rest may doe what they will till midnight; and then his Mate with his Larboord men, with a Psalme and a Prayer, releeves them till foure in the morning. And so from eight to twelve each other, except some flaw of winde come—some storme or gust—or some accident that requires the helpe of all hands, which commonly, after such good cheere, in most voyages doth happen.

For now *the wind veeres,* that is, it doth shift from point to point. Get your Starboord tacks aboord, and *tally* or hale off your Lee-Sheats. The Ship will not wayer [wear or veer]. Settle your maine Topsaile, veere a fadome of your sheat! *The wind veeres.* *Tally.*

The wind comes faire againe and a fresh gale. *Hale up the slatch of the Lee-boling.* By *Slatch* is meant the middle part of any rope hangs over boord. *Veere more sheat,* or, *a flowne sheat,* that is when they are not haled home to *Flowne.*

F   49

Fly.

the blocke. But when we say *Let fly the sheats,* then they let go amaine, which commonly is in some gust, lest they spend [see p. 51] their top-sailes, or if her quicke side[1] lie in the water, overset the ship.

A paire of courses.

A flowne Sheat is when shee goes before the wind, or *betwixt a paire of sheats,* or *all sailes drawing.* But *The wind shrinkes,*[2] that is when you must take in the Spret-saile and get the tacks aboord. *Hale close the maine Buling,* that is when your Tacks are close aboord. If you would saile against the wind or *keepe your owne,* that is, not to fall to lee-ward or goe backe againe, by halling off close your Bolings, you set your sailes so sharp as you can to lie close by a wind, thwarting it a league or two, or more or lesse, as you see cause, first on the one boord [tack] then on the other. This we call *Boording,* or *Beating it up upon a tacke in the Wind's Eye,* or *Bolting To and Againe;* but the longer [40] your boords are, the more you worke or gather into the wind. If a sudden flaw of wind should surprise you, when you would lower a yard so fast as you can, they call *Amaine!* But a crosse saile. [square-rigged ship] cannot come neerer the wind than six points; but a Carvell [caravel], whose sailes stand like a paire of Tailer's sheeres, will goe much neerer.

How to handle a Ship in a Storme.

It over-casts. We shall have wind, fowle weather. Settell your top sailes, take in the spret-saile, in with your top-sailes, lower the fore-saile, tallow [grease] under the parrels, brade up close all them sailes, lash sure the ordnance, strike your top-masts to the cap, make it sure with your sheep's feet.[3]

Try.

A storme. Let us lie at Trie[4] *with our maine course.*

[1] The quick side referred to the freeboard, or the distance from the top of the topmost plank to the water line; in this case, on the leeward side of the ship.   [2] Blows fitfully, or in gusts.

[3] A stay used in settling a top mast. See Smith, *An Accidence,* page. 16.

[4] In modern fore- and aft-rigged sailing craft, a triangular storm trysail is used.

That is to hale the tacke aboord, the sheat close aft, the boling set up, and the helme tied close aboord [amidships]. When that will not serve, then Try the mizen. If that split, or the storme grow so great she cannot beare it, then *Hull*, which is to beare no saile; but *to Strike a Hull*, is when they would lie obscurely in the Sea, or stay for some consort, lash sure the helme a'lee, and so a good ship will lie at ease *Under the Sea* [broadside to the sea], as wee terme it.

Hull.

Under the Sea.

If shee will *Weather Coile*,[1] and lay her head the other way without loosing a saile, that must bee done by bearing up the Helme, and then shee will drive nothing so farre to Leeward. They call it *Hulling* also in a calme swelling Sea, which is commonly before a storme, when they strike their sailes lest she should beat them in peeces against the mast by *Rowling*. We say a ship doth *Labour* much when she doth rowle much any way; but if she will neither Try nor Hull, then *Spoone*, that is, put her right before the wind. This way, although shee will rowle more than the other, yet if she be weake, it will not straine her any thing so much in the *Trough* of the Sea, which is the distance betwixt two waves or Billowes. If none of this will doe well, then she is in danger to *founder*, if not sinke. *Foundering* is when she will neither veere nor steare, the Sea will so over rake her, except you free out the water, she will lie like a log, and so consequently sinke.

Weather coile.

Rowling [rolling].
Labour.
Spoone.

Trough.

Founder.

To spend a Mast or Yard, is when they are broke by fowle weather, and to *Spring a Mast*, is when it is cracked in any place. [41]

To spend a mast.
Spring a mast.

In this extremity, he that doth cun [con] the ship cannot have too much judgement nor experience to *Try her Drift*, or *How she Capes*, which are two tearmes also used in the trials of the running or setting of currants.

---

[1] To turn the ship so that the stern is to windward, with all sails struck. This was a favourable trait. Most ships, especially those with a high stern, would not weather coil.

A Yoke.

A *Yoke* is [made] when the Sea is so rough as that men cannot govern the Helme with their hands, & then they sease a block to the Helme on each side at the end, & reeving two fal[l]s¹ thorow them like Gunner's Tackles, brings them to the ship's side; and so some being at the one side of the Tackle, some at the other, they steare her with much more ease than they can with a single rope with a double Turne about the Helme.

When the storme is past, though the wind may alter three or foure points of the compasse or more, yet the Sea for a good time will goe the same way. Then if your course be right against it, you shall meet it right a head,

A Head Sea.

so we call it *a Head Sea*. Sometimes when there is but little wind, there will come a contrary Sea, and presently the winde after it, wherby we may judge that from whence it came was much winde, for commonly before any great storme the Sea will come that way.

Now if the ship may runne on shore in ose [ooze] or mud, she may escape; or [if she] Billage on a rocke or Ancor's flooke, repaire her leake; but if she split or sinke, shee is a wracke² [wreck]. But seeing the storme

Hullocke.

decreaseth, let us trie if she will endure the *Hullocke* of a Saile, which sometimes is a peece of the mizen saile or some other little saile part opened, to keepe her head to the sea; but if yet shee would Weather Coile, wee will loose a Hullocke of her fore-saile and put the Helme a' weather, and it will bring her head where her sterne is. *Courage, my hearts!*

It cleares up, set your fore-saile! Now it is faire weather.

Lardge [large].
Laske.

*Out with all your sailes, goe lardge, or laske.*³ That is when

---

¹ That end of a rope running through a block, to which power is applied.

² As in *wrack and ruin*.

³ *Go large, lask, go roomy, put her roomy*, or *by a quartering*, or *large wind*, all have the same meaning.

we have a fresh gale or faire wind,[1] and all sailes drawing. But for more haste, unparrell[2] the mizen yard and lanch it, and the saile over her Lee quarter, and fit Giues [guys] at the further end to keepe the yard steady, and with a Boome, boome it out. This we call a *Goose-wing*.

Goosewing.

Who is at Helme there? Sirra, you must be amongst the Points!

Well Master, [42] *the Channell is broad enough, yet you cannot steare betwixt a paire of sheats.* Those are words of mockery betwixt the Cunner and the Stearesman.[3] But to proceed.

Get your Larboord Tackes aboord . . . Hale off your starboord sheats . . . Keepe your course upon the point you are directed, Port. He will lay her by the lee![4] The *Staies* or *Backe Staies,* that is when all the sailes flutter in the winde and are not kept full—that is, full of wind—they fall upon the masts and shrouds so that the ship goes a drift upon her broad side.

Fill the sailes, keepe full—full and by! Make ready to Tacke about!, is but for every man to stand to handle the sailes and ropes they must hale. *Tacke About* is to beare up the helme, and that brings her to *Stay,* all her sailes lying flat against the shrowds; then, as she turnes, wee say *Shee is Payed.* Then let rise your Lee-tacks and hale

[1] A wind from abaft the beam.

[2] To remove the parrels and breast-rope that hold the yard to the mast.

[3] Smith was reminded of this standard seaman's joke by some remarks of Mainwaring about masters who gave commands to the helmsman at every little yaw, " . . . which the sea-faring men love not, as being a kind of disgrace to their steerage. Then in mockage they will say, *sure the channel is so narrow he conds* [cons] *so thick . . .*" A little later Mainwaring says (*ibid.,* II, 130), ". . . if the ship go before a wind, or (as they term it), *betwixt two sheets . . .*"

[4] *Ibid.,* 178: "to bring her so that all her sails may lie against the masts and shrouds flat, and the wind to come right on her broadside, so that the ship will lie, as it were, stark still; or if she make any way, it will be with her broadside."

off your sheats, and trim all your sailes as they were before, which is, *Cast of[f] that Boling* (which was the weather boling), *and Hale up taught the other*, so all your Sheats, Brases and Tackes are trimmed by a winde [for sailing to windward] as before.

To Belay is to make fast the ropes in their proper *Round in.* places. *Round in* is when the wind larges [comes from abaft of the quarter], let rise the maine tacke and fore tacke and hale aft the fore sheat to the cat's head, and the maine sheat to the cubbridge head. This is *Rounding In*, *Rounding Aft.* or *Rounding Aft* the saile. The Sheats being there, they hale them downe to keepe them firme from flying up *Pasarado.* with a *Pasarado*, which is any rope wherewith wee hale downe the sheat's blockes of the maine or fore saile when they are haled aft, the clew of the maine saile to the Cubbridge head [forward] of the maine mast, and the clew of the fore saile to the Cat head. Doe this when the Ships Goes Large.

Observe. *Observe the Height*, that is at twelve a'clocke to take the height of the Sunne, or in the night, the North star; or in the forenoone and afternoone, if you misse these, by finding the Azimuth and Alnicanter [almacantar, see p. 93].

Dead water. *Dead Water* is the Eddie water [that] followes the sterne of the ship, not passing away so quickly as that *The Wake.* [which] slides by her sides. The *Wake* of a ship is the smooth water a' sterne, shewing the way shee hath [43] gone in the sea. By this we judge what way she doth make, for if the wake be right a' sterne, we know she makes good her way forwards; but if to Lee-ward a point or two, wee then thinke [she is] to the Lee-ward of her course. But shee is a nimble ship that in turning or tacking about will not fall to thee Lee-ward of her wake when shee hath weathered it [sailed to windward].

Disimbogue is to passe some narrow strait or currant into the maine Occan, out of some great Gulfe or Bay. A *Drift* is any thing floating in the sea that is of wood. *Rockweed* doth grow by the shore, and is a signe of land, yet it is oft found farre in the Sea.

Disimbogue.

A Drift.
Rockweed.

Lay the Ship by the Lee to trie the Dipsie Line!, which is a small line some hundred and fifty fadome [fathom] long, with a long plummet at the end, made hollow, wherein is put tallow that will bring up any gravell; which is first marked at twenty fadome, and after increased by tens to the end; and those distinguished by so many small knots upon each little string that is fixed at the marke thorow the strouds[1] or middest of the line, shewing it is so many times ten fadome deepe where the *plummet* doth rest from drawing the line out of your hand. This is onely used in deepe water when we thinke we approach the shore, for in the maine sea, at 300 fadomes we finde no bottome.

Dipsie Line
[*deep sea line*].

Bring the ship to rights!, that is, againe under saile as she was.

Some use *Log line*, and a minute glasse to know what way shee makes, but that is so uncertaine, it is not worth the labour to trie it.

Log line

One to the top to looke out for land!

The man cries out *Land to!*, which is just so farre as a *Kenning*, or a man may discover, descrie, or see the land. And *to lay a land* is to saile from it just so farre as you can see it. *A Good Land fall* is when we fall just with our reckoning; if otherwise, a *Bad Land fall*. But however how it beares, set it by the compasse, and bend your Cables to the Anchors.

Land to.
Kenning.
To lay a land.
Good land fall.
Bad land fall.

A Head land, or a *Point of land* doth lie further out at sea than the rest. A *Land marke* is any Mountaine,

A head land.
A Point.
Land marke.

---

[1] Another inversion of *u* and *n*. *Strond* is the obsolete form of *strand*.

To raise a land.
To make land.
Rocke, Church, Wind-mill or the like, that the Pilot can know, by comparing one by another, how they beare by the compasse.

A Reach.
A Reach [44] is the distance of two points so farre as you can see them in a right line, as White Hall and London Brid[g]e, or White Hall and the end of Lambeth towards Chelsey.

Sounding Line.
Fetch the Sounding line. This is bigger than the Dipsie Line, and is marked at two fadome next the lead with a peece of blacke leather, at three fadome the like, but slit; at 5 fadome with a peece of white cloth, at 7 fadome with a peece of red in a peece of white leather, at 15 with a white cloth, etc.

The Lead.
The sounding lead is six or seven pound weight, and neere a foot long. He that doth heave this lead stands by the horse [see p. 25], or in the chaines, and doth sing "Fadome by the marke 5 c. and a shaftment[1] less 4.0." This is to finde where the ship may saile by the depth of

Fowle water.
the water. *Fowle Water* is when she comes into shallow water where shee raises the sand or ose with her way, yet not touch the ground; but shee cannot feele her helme so well as in deepe water.

Beare in.
When a ship sailes with a large wind towards the land, or a faire wind into a harbour, we say *She beares in with the land or harbour.* And when she would not come neere the land, but goeth more Roome-way [roomy][2] than her

Beare off.
cou[r]se, wee say *She Beares off.* But a ship boord *Beare off!* is used to every thing you would thrust from you.

Beare up.
Hold off.
Beare up, is to bring the ship to goe large or before the wind. To *Hold off* is when we heave the Cable at the Capsterne, if it be great and stiffe or slimie with ose, it

Surges.
surges or slips backe unlesse they keep it close to the

---

[1] Shaftment: the breadth of a man's hand plus the length of his extended thumb; about six inches.

[2] Rooming: the navigable water to the leeward of a vessel. A ship sailing more *roomy* than her course is sailing in the *rooming.*

whelps, and then they either hold it fast with nippers, or brings it to the Jeare Capsterne, and this is called *Holding Off*. [See p. 9].

As you approach the shore, shorten your sailes. When you are in harbour, take in your sailes and come to an anchor, wherein much judgement is required; [as] to know well the soundings, if it be *Nealed to*, that is, deepe water close aboord the shore, or shallow; or if the lee under-the-weather shore, or the lee shore[1] be sandy, clay, osie or fowle and rockie ground; but the Lee shore all men would shun that can avoid it. Or a *Roade*, which is an open place neere the shore; or the *Offing*, which is the open Sea from the shore, or the middest of any great streame is called [45] the *Offing*. *Land Locke* is when the land is round about you.

Neale To.

A Roade.
Offing.

Land locked.

Now the ship is said *to Ride* so long as the Anchors doe hold and *comes not home*.[2] To *Ride a great Roade* is when the winde hath much power. They will strike their top masts, and the yards, alongst ships, and the deeper the water is, it requires more Cable. When wee have rid in any distresse, we say *We have rid hawse full*, because the water broke into the hawses.

To *Ride betwixt Wind and Tide* is when the wind & tide are contrary & of equall power, which will make her rowle extremely, yet not straine much the cable. To *Ride thwart* is to ride with her side to the tide, and then she never straines it. To *Ride Apike* [a'peak] is to pike [peak][3] your yards when you ride amongst many ships.

To Ride.
Ride a great Roade.

Ride a' stresse.

Ride betwixt Wind and tide.
Ride thwart tide.

Ride a' pike.

[1] Lee shore: the shore toward which the wind blows from the sea was considered very dangerous, since square-rigged ships of that day did not work well to windward, and were apt to be driven ashore by wind and water movement. A weather shore was considered safe. In the lee of, or *under the weather shore* was therefore a safe berth. The modern expression "under the weather" stems from this.

[2] The ship does not drag its anchor.

[3] To set the yards with one end brought down close to the shrouds, the other being raised high.

Ride crosse.

To *Ride Acrosse* is to hoise the maine and fore yards to the hounds [see p. 19], and topped alike.

Sewed.
Sew.

When the water is gone and the ships lies dry, we say, *She is Sewed.* If her head but lie dry, *She is Sewed a Head*; but if she cannot all lie dry, *She Cannot Sew There.*

Water borne.
Water Line.

Water Borne is when there is no more water than will just beare her from the ground. The *Water Line* is to that Bend or place she should swim in when she is loaded.

To More [moor].

Lastly, *to More* a ship is to lay out her anchors as is most fit for her to ride by, and the wayes are divers; as first, to *More a faire Berth*[1] from any annoiance. To

More crosse.

More a crosse is to lay one anchor to one side of the streame, and the other to the other right against [opposite] one another, and so they beare equally ebbe and flood.

More alongst.

To *More Alongst* is to lay an anchor amidst the streame ahead, and another asterne, when you feare driving a

Water Shot.

shore. *Water Shot* is to more quartering betwixt both, nether crosse nor alongst the tide. In an open rode they will more [heading] that way they thinke the wind will

More Proviso.

come the most to hurt them. To more *a'Proviso*, is to have one anchor in the river, and a hawser a'shore, which is mored with her head a shore; otherwise two cables is the least, and foure cable the best to more by.

---

[1] Clear of any obstructions.

Chapter X

Proper tearmes for the Winds, Ebbes, Floods and Eddies, with their definitions, and an estimate of the depth of the Sea, by the height of the Hils and the largeness of the Earth.

When there is not a breath of wind stirring, it is *a Calme*, or a *Starke calme*. A *breze* is a wind [*that*] blowes out of the Sea, and commonly in faire weather beginneth about nine in the morning, and lasteth till neere night. So likewise all the night it is from the shore, which is called a *Turnado*[1] or a *Sea-turne*, but this is but upon such coasts where it bloweth thus most certainly, except it be a storme or very fowle weather, as in *Barbaria* [N.W. Africa], *Ægypt*, and the most of the Levant. We have such Brezes in most hot countreys in Summer, but they are very uncertaine.

A Calme.
A Bre[e]ze.

A *fresh Gale* is that [which] doth presently blow after a calme, when the wind beginneth to quicken or blow. A *faire Loome Gale* is the best to saile in, because the Sea goeth not high, and we beare out all our sailes. A *stiffe Gale* is so much wind as our top-sailes can endure to beare. An *Eddie wind* is checked by the saile, a mountaine, turning, or any such thing that makes it returne backe againe. *It over blowes* when we can beare no top-sailes. A *flaw of wind* is a *Gust* which is very violent upon a sudden, but quickly endeth.

A fresh gale.
A Loome gale.

Eddie [eddy] wind.
It over blowes.
A Gust.

[1] A land breeze, not to be confused with a tornado.

A Spout.

A *Spout* in the West Indies commonly falleth in those Gusts, which is, as it were, a small river falling entirely from the clouds, like out of our water Spouts,[1] which make the Sea where it falleth rebound [47] in flashes [splashes or waves] exceeding high. *Whirle winds*

A whirle wind.

runneth round, and bloweth divers wayes at once. A

A Storme.
A Tempest.
A Mounsoune
[monsoon].

storme is knowne to every one not to bee much lesse than a *tempest*, that will blow downe houses, and trees up by the roots. A *Mounsoune* is a constant wind in the East Indies, that bloweth alwayes three moneths together one way, and the next three moneths the contrary way. A

A Hericano
[hurricane].

Hericano is so violent in the West Indies, it will continue three, foure or five weekes,[2] but they have it not past once in five, six or seven yeeres; but then it is with such extremity that the Sea flies like raine,[3] and the waves so high, they over flow the low grounds by the Sea in so much that ships have been driven over tops of high trees there growing, many leagues into the land, and there left; as was Captaine *Francis Nelson*,[4] a Englishman and an excellent Sea man, for one.

Becalmed.

We say a *calme sea* or *Becalmed*, when it is so smooth the ship move very little, and the men leap over boord to

A Rough Sea.
An over-growne
Sea.
Surges.
The Rut of the
Sea.

swim. A *Rough Sea* is when the waves grow high. An *over-growne Sea*, when the *surges* and billowes goe highest. The *Rut of the Sea*, where it doth dash against any thing. And the *Roaring of the Sea* is most commonly observed a shore a little before a storme, or after a storme.

Flood is when the water beginneth to rise, which is

[1] It is exactly the opposite; a whirling up-current of warm, moist air, the outside of which is cloud-like, giving it the same funnel shape as a tornado or whirlwind ashore.

[2] Smith apparently never experienced a hurricane, as this description is in error; while the total life of a hurricane may be 3 or 4 weeks, it takes only 3 or 4 days for the entire system to pass a given point.

[3] This description tallies closely with Beaufort number 12 or higher.

[4] Commander of the *Phoenix*, which supplied Jamestown in 1608.

young flood as we call it; then *quarter flood, halfe flood, full Sea, still water,* or, *high water;* so when it *Ebbes: quarter ebbe, halfe ebbe, three quarter ebbe, low water* or *dead low water,* every one doth know; and also that as at a *spring tide* the Sea or water is at the highest, so at a *Neape tide* it is at the lowest.

The Roaring of the Sea.
Floods and ebbes.

This word *Tide* is common both to Flood and Ebbe; for you say as well *tide of ebbe* as *tide of flood,* or a *windward Tide* (when the Tide runnes against the streame) as a *Lee-warde Tide;* that is when the wind and the Tide goeth both one way, which makes the water as smooth as the other rough. To *Tide over*[1] to a place is to goe over with the Tide of ebbe or flood, and stop the contrary by anchoring till the next Tide. Thus you may worke against the wind if it over blow not.

A Tide of ebbe.
A Tid⸱ of flood.
A windward tide.
A Lee-ward tide.
To Tide over.

A *Tide gate* is where [48] the tide runneth strongest. It flowes *Tide* and *halfe Tide,* that is, it will be halfe flood by the shore before it begin to flow in the channell; for although the Tide of flood run aloft, yet the Tide of ebbe runnes close by the ground.

A Tide gate.
Tide and halfe Tide.

An *Eddie tide* is where the water doth runne backe contrary to the tide, that is, when some headland or great point in a River hindereth the free passage of the streame, that causeth the water on the other side the point to turne round by the shore as in a circle, till it fall into the tide againe.

Eddie Tide.

As touching the reasons of ebbes and floods, and to know how far it is to the bottome of the deepest place of the Sea, I will not take upon me to discourse of, as knowing the same to be the secrets of God, unrevealed to man; only I will set downe a Philosophicall speculation of divers men's opinions touching the depth of the Sea, which I hope will not be thought much impertinent to the subject of this booke by the judicious Reader.

[1] This is the origin of the modern colloquialism.

The height of mountaines perpendicular.

Fabianus in *Plinie*, and *Cleomides*, conceived the depth of the Sea to be fifteene furlongs, that is, a mile and 7/8 parts. *Plutarch* compared it equall to the highest mountaines. *Scallinger* and others conceited the hils farre surpassed the deepnesse of the Sea, and that in few places it is more than a hundred paces in depth. It may bee hee meant in some narrow Seas, but in the maine Ocean, experience hath taught us it is much more than twice so much, for I have sounded 300 fadome, yet found no ground.

Eratosthenes, in *Theon*, that great Mathematitian, writeth the highest mountain perpendicular is but ten furlongs, that is, one mile and a quarter. Also *Dicæarcus* affirmeth this to be the height of the hill *Pelius* in *Thessalia*; but *Xenagoras*, in *Plutarch*, observed the height of [Mount] *Olimpus*, in the same region, to be twenty paces more, which is 1270 paces. But surely all those meane onely those mountaines in or about *Greece*, where they lived and were best acquainted; but how these may compare with the Alps in *Asia*, *Atlas* in *Africa*, *Caucasus* in *India*, the *Andes* in *Peru*, and divers others, hath not yet beene examined.

The height of the hils compared with the super- ficies of the earth and depth of the Sea.

[49] But whatsoever the hils may be above the superficies [surface] of the earth, many hold opinion the Sea is much deeper; who suppose that the earth at the first framing was in the superficies regular and sphericall, as the holy Scriptures directs us to beleeve, because the water covered and compassed all the face of the earth. Also that the face of the earth was equal to that of the Sea. *Damascen* noteth, that the unevennesse and irregularity which now is seene in the earth's superficies was caused by taking some parts out of the upper face of the earth in sundry places to make it more hollow, and lay[-ing] them in other places to make it more convex, or by raising up some part and depressing others to make roome and receit [receipt: reservoir] for the Sea, that mutation

being wrought by the power of the word of the Lord: *Let the waters be gathered into one place that the dry Land may appeare.*

As for *Aquinas, Dionysius, Catharianus,* and some Divines that conceited there was no mutation, but [that] a violent accumulation of the waters, or heaping them up on high, is unreasonable; because it is against nature that water, being a flexible and a ponderous body, so to consist and stay it self, and not fall to the lower parts about it, where in nature there is nothing to hinder it; or, if it be restrained supernaturally by the hand and bridle of Almighty God lest it should over-whelme and drowne all the land, it must follow that God, even in the very institution of nature, imposed a perpetuall violence upon nature. And this with all, that at the Deluge there was no necessity to breake up the springs of the deepe and to open the cattaracts of Heaven, and powre downe water continually so many daies and nights together, seeing only the with-drawing of that hand, or letting goe of that bridle which straineth the water, would presently have overwhelmed all.

But both by Scriptures, the experience of Navigators, and reason, in making estimation of the depth of the Sea, reckon not onely the height of the hils above the common superficies of the earth, but the height of all the dry land above the superficies of the Sea; because the whole masse [50] of earth that now appeareth above the waters, being taken, as it were, out of the places which the waters now possesse, must be equall to the place out of which it was taken. So consequently it seemeth that the height or elevation of the one should answer the descending or depth of the other, and therefore in estimating the depth of the Sea, wee consider not onely the erection of the hils above the ordinary land, but the advantage of the dry land above the Sea, [by] which latter I meane the height of the ordinary maine land, excluding the hils, which

How all the hils and dry land above the superficies of the Sea hath made roome for the Sea, therefore they are in equall height & depth.

63

properly answer the extraordinary deepes and whirle-pooles in the Sea. The rest is held more in large Continents above the Sea than that of the hils is above the land, for that the plain face of the dry land is not level or equally distant from the Center, but hath a great descent towards the Sea and a rising towards the mid-land parts, although it appeare not plainly to the eye; yet to reason it is most manifest, because we find that part of the earth the Sea covereth descendeth lower and lower towards the Sea. For the Sea, which touching the upper face of it is knowne by nature to be levell and evenly distant from the center, is observed to wax deeper & deeper the further one saileth from the shore towards the maine Ocean; even so [as] in that part which is uncovered, the streamings of Rivers on all sides from the mid-land parts towards the Sea, sliding from the higher to the lower, declareth so much, whose courses are some 1000 or 2000 miles. In which declination *Pliny*, in his derivation of water, requireth one cubit of declining in 240 foot of proceeding. But *Columella, Viturnius, Paladius* and others, in their con-duction of waters require somewhat lesse; namely, that in the proceeding of 200 foot forward, there should bee allowed one foot of descending downeward, which yet in the course of 1000 miles (as [the] *Danubius, Volgha* or *Indies* [Danube, Volga, Indus], *etc.*, [which] have so much or more) ~~which~~ will make five miles of descent in per-pendicular account, and in the course of 2000 or more— as *Nilus* [Nile], *Niger*, and the River of the Amazons— have 10 miles or more of the like descent. [51]

These are not taken as rules of necessity, as though water could not runne without that advantage. For that respect, the conveyers of waters in these times content themselves with one inch in 600 foot, as *Philander* and *Viturnius* observed. But [it] is rather under a rule of commodity for expedition and wholsomnesse of water so conveyed, lest resting too long in pipes, it should contract

That there is small difference betwixt the springs first rising out of the earth and their falling into the Sea.

The determina-tion of these questions.

A Murderer, an iron breech-loading anti-personnel weapon. Note the swivel with its pintel below; also the breech block, held in place by an iron wedge.

The Seamans Secrets.

terly placing of the staff to the eye, which demonstration I have found, and have had the Instrument in practise, aswel under the Sunt, as in other Climates, but because it hath a large demonstration, with manifold uses, I here omit to manifest the same, purposing to write a particular Treatise thereof, notwithstanding his Forme and use, by picture I have thought good to expresse.

This staff is a yard long, having two half crosses, the one circular, the other strait, the longest not 14 inches, yet this staff doth contain the whole 90 degrees, the shortest degree being an inch and ½ long, wherein the minuts are particularly & very sensibly laid down, by which staff not regarding the parallax of your sight, nor looking upon the Sun, but onely upon the Horizon, the Suns height is most precisely known, aswel and as easily in the Zenith, as in any other part of the heaven. As which Instrument (in my opinion) the Seaman shall not find any so good, and in all Climates of so great certainty, the Invention and demonstration whereof I may boldly challenge to appertain unto my self (as a portion of the Talent which God hath bestowed upon me) I hope without abuse or offence to any.

A 90° backstaff in use. Illustration from The Seamans Secrets *by John Davis, 1595.*

A Table of proportion for the weight and shooting of great Ordance.

	The names of the great Peeces.	The height of the peeces. Inches.	The weight of the peeces. Pound.	The weight of the shot. Pound.	The weight of the powder. Pound.	The bredth of the Ladle. Inches.	The length of the Ladle. Inches.	2400.li. of powder makes Peeces.	Shot point blanke shot in a Paces.	Shot ran-dome in Paces.
1	A Canon Rovall.	$8\frac{1}{2}$	8000	66	30	$13\frac{3}{4}$	$24\frac{1}{4}$	80	16	1930
2	A Canon.	8	6000	60	27	12	24	85	17	2000
3	A Canon Sarpentine.	$7\frac{1}{2}$	5500	$53\frac{1}{2}$	25	$10\frac{1}{2}$	$23\frac{1}{2}$	96	20	2000
4	A Baftard Canon.	7	4500	$41\frac{1}{4}$	20	10	$23\frac{1}{3}$	120	18	1800
5	A demy Canon.	$6\frac{1}{2}$	4000	$30\frac{1}{4}$	18	$9\frac{1}{2}$	$23\frac{1}{4}$	133	17	1700
6	A Canon Petro.	6	3000	$24\frac{1}{4}$	14	9	23	171	16	1600
7	A Culvering.	$5\frac{1}{2}$	4500	$17\frac{1}{2}$	12	$8\frac{1}{2}$	$22\frac{1}{3}$	200	20	2500
8	A Bafilifco.	5	4000	$15\frac{1}{4}$	10	7	22	240	25	3000
9	A demy Culvering.	$4\frac{1}{2}$	3400	$9\frac{1}{2}$	8	$6\frac{1}{2}$	21	300	20	2500
10	A baftard Culvering.	4	3000	7	$6\frac{1}{4}$	6	20	388	18	1800
11	A Sacre.	$3\frac{1}{2}$	1400	$5\frac{1}{2}$	$5\frac{1}{4}$	$5\frac{1}{2}$	18	490	17	1700
12	A Minion.	$3\frac{1}{4}$	1000	4	4	$4\frac{1}{2}$	17	600	16	1600
13	A Faulcon.	$2\frac{1}{2}$	660	$2\frac{1}{4}$	$2\frac{1}{4}$	$4\frac{1}{4}$	15	1087	15	1500
14	A Faulconet.	$2\frac{1}{4}$	800	3	3	$4\frac{1}{4}$	15	800	15	1500
15	A Faulconet.	2	500	$1\frac{1}{4}$	$1\frac{1}{2}$	$3\frac{3}{4}$	$11\frac{1}{4}$	1950	14	1400
16	A Sarpentine.	$1\frac{1}{2}$	400	$\frac{1}{2}$	$\frac{1}{3}$	$2\frac{1}{2}$	10	7200	13	1300
17	A Rabonet.	1	300		$\frac{1}{2}$	$1\frac{1}{2}$	6	4800	12	1000

Thefe Peeces be: moft fervuiceable for battery being within 80. paces to their marke, which is the chiefe of their forces.

Thefe Peeces be good and alfo fer-uiceable to be mixt with the above Ordnance for battery to peeces being crofs with the reft, as alfo fit for Caftles, Forts, and walls to be planted, and for defence.

Thefe Peeces are good and feruice-able for the field, and moft ready for defence.

some unwholsome condition, or else through the slacknesse of motion, or long closenesse, or banishment from
the aire, gather some aptnesse and disposition to
putrifie.

Although I say, such excesse of advantage as in the
artificiall conveyance of waters the forenamed Authors
require, be not of necessity exacted in the naturall
derivation of them. Yet certaine it is that the descent of
rivers being continually, and their course long, and in
many places swift, and in some places headlong and *Note the differ-*
furious—the differences of height of advantage cannot *ence betwixt the*
be great betwixt the springs of the rivers and their out lets *springs of the*
—betwixt the first rising out of the earth and their *rivers and their*
falling into the Sea; unto which declinity of land seeing *falling into the*
the deepenesse of the Sea in proportion answer, as I before *Sea is not great.*
declared, and not onely to the height of the hils.

It is concluded, that the deepenesse to bee much more
than the Philosophers commonly reputed. And although
the deepnesse of the Sardinian Sea, which *Aristotle* saith
was the deepest of the Mediterranean, [was] recorded by
Posidonius in *Strabo* to have beene found but 1000
fadome (which is but a mile and a fifth part), and the
greatest bredth not past 600 miles—then seeing if in so
narrow a Sea it be so deepe, what may we esteeme the
maine Ocean [the Atlantic] to be, that in many places is
five times so broad, seeing the broader the Seas are, if
they be intire and free from Ilands, they are answerably
observed to be the deeper?

If you desire any further satisfaction, read the first
part of *Purchas his Pilgrimage*,[1] where you may read how
to find all those Authors at large. Now because he hath

[1] Samuel Purchas, *Pilgrimage*, London, 1613. After the table of
contents a catalogue of the authors quoted was printed, and it is to
this that Smith refers. The dissertation was also published in *Hakluytus
Posthumus, or Purchas his Pilgrimes* (1625–1626), Glasgow (1904–
1907), I, 337–43.

taken neere 100 times as much from me, I have made bold to borrow this from him, seeing he hath sounded such deepe waters for this our Ship [52] to saile in; being a Gentleman whose person I loved, and whose memory and vertues I will ever honour.

Chapter XI

Proper Sea tearmes belonging to the good or bad condition of Ships; how to finde them and amend them.

A Ship that will try, hull, and ride well at Anchor, we call a *wholsome Ship*. A long Ship that drawes much water will doe all this, but if she draw much water and be short, she may hull well, but neither try nor ride well. If she draw little water and be long, she may try and ride well, but never hull well, which is called an *unwholsome ship*.

The *howsing* in of a Ship is when shee is past the bredth of her bearing, she is brought in narrow to her upper workes. It is certaine this makes her wholsome in the Sea without rowling, because the weight of her Ordnance doth counterpoise her bredth under water; but it is not so good in a man of warre, because it taketh away a great deale of her roome. Nor will her tacks ever so well come aboord as if she were laid out aloft, and not *flaring*, which is when she is a little howsing in neere the water, and then the upper worke doth hang over againe, and is laid out broder aloft. This makes a Ship more roomy aloft for men to use their armes in; but Sir *Walter Rawleigh's*[1] proportion, which is to be pro-

A wholsome Ship.

An unwholsome Ship.

Howsing [housing] a Ship.

Flaring.

---

[1] In 1614 Raleigh published the first two books of his projected *History of the World*, which had been registered in Stationers' Hall three years earlier. In Lib. 5, chap. I, vi, he mentions an unfinished treatise, "The Art of War at Sea." He had written this for Henry, Prince of Wales, but had stopped working on it on Henry's death in 1612. There is a letter "to Henery, Prince of Wales" which may have been part of this in *The Life of Sir Walter Raleigh*, Edward Edwards, London, 1868 [two vols., I, 330].

portionally wrought to her other worke, is the best;
because the counterpoise on each side doth make her
swimme perpendicular or straight, and consequently
steady, which is the best.

If a ship be narrow, and her bearing either not laid out
[53] enough, or too low, then you must make her broader
and her bearing the higher by ripping off the plankes two
or three strakes [seams] under water, and as much above,
and put other Timbers upon the first, and then put on
the plankes upon those Timbers. This will make her beare
a better saile, but it is a hindrance to her sailing. This is
Cranke side.　to be done when a Ship is *cranke sided*[1] and will beare no
Furring.　saile, and is called *Furring*. Note also that when a Ship
hath a deepe Keele, it doth keepe her from rowling. If
she be floty [floaty],[2] and her keele shallow, put on
another keele under the first to make it deeper, for it
will make her hold more in the water. This wee call a
A false Keele.　*false Keele*. Likewise, if her stem be too flat, to make her
Gripe.　cut water the better and not *Gripe* (which is when shee
will not keepe a winde well),[3] fix another stem before it;
A false stem.　and that is called a *false stem*, which will make her rid[e]
[with] more way and beare a better saile.

The runne [run].　Also the *Run* of a ship is as much to be regarded, for
if it be too short and too full below, the water comes but
slowly to the Rudder because the force of it is broken by
her bredth; and then to put a false stern post to lengthen
her is the next remedy. But to lengthen her is better, for
when [sic: then] a Ship comes off handsomly by degrees,
and her Tuck doth not lye too low, which will hinder
the water from comming swiftly to the Rudder, [and]
makes her [so] she cannot steare well; and they are called,
A good runne.　as they are, a *good runne* or a *bad*.
A bad runne.

When a Ship hath lost a peece of her Keele, and that
we cannot come well to mend it, you must pitch [patch]

---

[1] Unstable due to a high centre of gravity, as opposed to *stiff*.
[2] Drawing little water.　　　[3] Sail well to windward.

a new peece unto it and bind it with a *Stirrop*, which   *A S[t]irrup.*
is an iron [that] comes round about it and the Keele, up
to the other side of the Ship, whereto it is strongly nailed
with Spikes.

Her *Rake* also may be a defect, which is so much of the   *Her Rake.*
Hull as by a perpendicular line the end of the Keele is
from the setting-on of the stem—so much as is without
that forward on; and in like manner the setting in of her
stem [sic: stern] Post. Your French men gives great
Rakes forwards on, which makes her give good way and
keepe a good wind, but if she have not a full bow she will
pitch her head extremely in the Sea. If shee have but a
small Rake, [55][1] she is so bluffe that the Seas meets her
so suddenly upon the Bowes, shee cannot cut the water
much. But the longer a ship is, the fuller should be her
Bow; but the meane is the best.

The *Looming* of a ship is her prospective, that is, as she   *Loome.*
doth shew great or little. Her *water draught* is so many
foot as she goes in the water, but the Ships that drawes
most water are commonly the most wholsome; but the
least draught goes best but rolls most. And we say a Ship
doth *Heeld* on Starboord or Larboord, that is, to that   *Heeld [heel].*
side shee doth leane most.

To *Overset* or *Overthrow* a ship is by bearing too much   *Overset.*
saile, you bring her Keele upwards, or on shore over-   *Overthrow.*
throw her by grounding her, so that she falls upon one
side; and we say a Ship is *Walt*[2] when shee is not *stiffe*,   *Walt.*
and hath not Ballast enough in her to keepe her stiffe.
And *wall reared*, when she is right [straight] built up   *Wall reared.*
after shee comes to her bearing. It makes her ill shapen
and unseemely, but it gives her within much roome, and
she is very wholsome if her bearing be well laid out.

The Masting of a Ship is much to be considered, and

[1] Pagination is incorrect. In the original edition pages 54 and 55
are juxtaposed.   [2] Walt is synonymous for crank-sided.

will much cause her to saile well or ill, as I have related in *The Masting a Ship* [see p. 18].

Iron Sicke.

Iron Sicke is when the Bolts, Spikes or Nailes are so eaten with rust, they stand hollow in the plankes, and so makes her leake; the which to prevent, they use to put lead over all the bolt heads under water.

Trim.

Lastly, the *trimming* of a ship doth much amend or impaire her sailing, and so alter her condition. To finde her trim, that is, how she will saile best, is by trying her sailing with another Ship so many glasses, trimmed a head and so many a sterne, and so many upon an even Keele; also the easing of her Masts and Shrouds, for some ships will saile much better when they are slacke than when they are taught. [54]

Chapter *XII*

Considerations for a Sea Captaine in the choise of his Ship, and in placing his Ordnance; in giving Chase, Boording and entering a man of warre like himselfe, or a defending Merchant man.

In Land service we call a Man of Warre a Souldier either on foot or horse, and at Sea, a Ship; which, if she be not as well built, conditioned and provided, as neere fitting such an imploiment as may be, she may prove (either) as a horseman that knoweth not how to hold his raines, keepe his seat in his saddle and stirrops, carry his body, nor how to helpe his horse with leg and spur in a curvet,[1] gallop or stop; or as an excellent horsemen that knoweth all this, mounted upon a Jade that will doe nothing—which were he mounted according to his experience, hee would doe more with that one than halfe a dozen of the other, though as well provided as himselfe. But I confesse, every horseman canot mount himselfe alike, neither every Seaman ship himselfe as he would; I meane not for outward ornament, which the better they are, the lesse to be disliked—for there cannot be a braver sight than a ship in her bravery—but of a competent sufficiency as the businesse requireth.

But were I to chuse a ship for my self, I would have her saile well, yet strongly built, her decks flush and flat,

How to chuse a Ship fit to make a man-of-warre.

---

[1] A leaping manoeuvre in fancy horsemanship.

and so roomy that men might passe with ease; her Bow
and chase [stern] so Gall[e]y-like[1] contrived, should beare
as many Ordnances as with conveniency she could, for
that alwaies commeth most to fight; [56] and so stiffe,
she should beare a stiffe saile, and beare out her lower
tier [of guns] in any reasonable weather. Neither should
her Gunroome be unprovided; nor manned like a
Merchantman, which if they be double manned, that is,
to have twise so many men as would saile her, they think
it is too many in regard of the charge; yet to speake
true, there is few Merchant Ships in the world [that]
doth any way exceed ours. And those men they entertaine
in good voiages have such good pay, and such acquaintance
one with another in shipping themselves, that thirty or
forty of them would trouble a man of warre with three
or foure times their number, manned with prest[2] men,
being halfe of them scarce [able to] hale Boulings—yea,
and many times a Pirat, who are commonly the best
manned—but they fight only for wealth, not for honour
nor revenge, except they bee extremely constrained. But
such a Ship as I have spoken of, well manned with rather
too many than too few, with all sufficient Officers, Shot,
Powder, Victual and all their appurtenances—in my
opinion might well passe muster for a man of warre.

His reward that
first discries a
Ship, or enters a
prize.

Now being at Sea, the tops are seldome without one
or other to looke out for purchase [prey], because hee that
first discries a saile, if she prove [a] prize,[3] is to have a
good su[i]te of Aparell, or so much money as is set downe
by order for his reward; as also he that doth first enter
a Ship, there is a certaine reward allowed him.

When wee see a Ship alter her course, and useth all
the meanes she can to fetch you up, you are the *chase*,

[1] Galleys, which were rowed by slaves or convicts, had flush
decks.
[2] Men impressed into service by force.
[3] A captured ship.

72

and hee the *chaser*. In giving chase or chasing, or to escape being chased, there is required an infinite judgement and experience, for there is no rule for it; but the shortest way to fetch up your chase is the best. [When chasing:] if you bee too lee-ward, get all your Tacks aboord and shape your course as he doth, to meet him at the neerest angle you can. Then he must either alter his course and Tacke as you Tacke, as neere the wind as he can lye to keepe his owne till night, and then strike a-Hull [see p. 51], that you may not descry him by his sailes, or doe his best to lose you in the darke; for looke, how[-ever] much he falls to lee-ward, hee falls so much in [57] your way.

How to give chase, and escape the chaser.

If he be right ahead of you, that is called a *sterne chase*; if you weather him [get to his windward]—for every man in chasing doth seeke to get the weather, because you cannot boord him except you weather him— he will laske, or goe large [see p. 52]. If you gather on him that way, hee will trie you before the wind; then if your ordnance cannot reach him, if he can out-strip you, he is gone. But suppose you are to wind-ward: if hee clap close by a [sail close to the] wind and there goes a head sea, and yours a lee-ward ship,[1] if you doe the like, your ship will so beat against the Sea, she will make no way; therefore you must goe a little more large, though you chase under his lee till you can run ahead.

Boord and Boord is when two ships lie together side by side. But hee that knoweth how to defend himselfe and worke well will so cun his ship as [to] force you to enter upon his quarter, which is the highest part of the ship, and but the mizen shrouds to enter by, from whence he may do you much hurt with little danger, except you fire him (which a pirat will never do, neither sink you, if he can chuse, except you be able to force him to defend

Boord [board] & boord.

---

[1] A ship that cannot sail well to windward, and drifts to the leeward of its course.

himselfe). But in a Sea fight wee call *Boording* in *Boording* where wee can. The greatest advantage for your Ordnance is to boord him thwart the hawse, because you may use all the ordnance you have on one side, and she onely them in her prow.

Boording &
entering a ship.

But the best and safest boording for entring is on the bow, but you must be carefull to cleare the decks with burning granados [grenades], fire-pots [see p. 87], poutches of powder, to which give fire by a Gunpowder match [fuse], to prevent [their making] traines[1] to the

Powder chests.

powder chest; which are long boards joyned like a triangle, with divers broad ledges on either side, wherein lieth [gun-powder and] as many peeble [pebble] stones or beatch [beach stones] as can there lie. Those being fired will make all cleare before them. Besides, in an extremity a man would rather blow up the quarter decke, halfe decke, fore castle or any thing, than bee taken by him he knows a mortall enemy, and commonly there is more men lost in entering (if the chase stand to her defence) in an instant, than in a long fight boord and boord, if she be provided of her [58] close fights [see below]. I confesse, the charging upon trenches, and the entrances of a breach in a rampire [rampart] are attempts as desperate as a man would thinke could be performed; but he that hath tried himselfe as oft in the entring [of] a resisting ship as I have done—both them & the other—he would surely confesse there is no such dangerous service ashore as a resolved, resolute fight at sea.

A ship's *Close Fights* are smal ledges of wood laid crosse one another like the grates of iron in a prison's window, betwixt the maine mast and the fore mast, & are called *Gratings*; or *Nettings*, as is said, which are made of small ropes, much in like manner covered with a saile, the which to undoe is to heave a kedger, or fix a grapling

[1] Powder train: a fuse made by laying a path of gunpowder along the deck.

into them tied in a rope (but a chaine of iron is better), and shearing off, will teare it in peeces if the rope and anchor hold. Some have used *sheare hookes*, which are hookes like sickels fixed in the ends of the yards' armes, that if a ship under saile come to boord her, those sheares will cut her shrouds and spoile her tackling; but they are so subject to breake their owne yards, and cut all the ropes comes from the top-sailes, they are out of request [demand].

To conclude, if a ship bee open, presently to boord her is the best way to take her. But if you see your chase strip himselfe into fighting sailes—that is, to put out his colours in the poope, his flag in the maine top, his streamers or pendants at the ends of his yards' armes, furle his spret-saile, pike his mizen, and sling his maine yard— provide your self to fight. Now because I would not bee tedious in describing a fight at Sea, I have troubled you with this short preamble that you may the plainlier understand it. [59]

Evident signes that a chase will fight.

75

Chapter XIII

How to manage a fight at Sea, with the proper tearmes in a fight largely expressed, and the ordering of a Navy at Sea.

For this master peece of this worke, I confesse I might doe better to leave it to every particular man's conceit as it is, or those of longer practice or more experience; yet *Many bookes of* because I have seene many bookes of the Art of Warre *the Art of War* by land, and never any for the Sea—seeing all men so *for the land,* silent in this most difficult service, and there are so many *none for the sea.* young Captaines and others that desire to be Captaines, who know very little or nothing at all to any purpose—for their better understanding I have proceeded thus farre.

Now for this that followes—what I have seene, done and conceived by my small experience, I referre me to their friendly constructions and well advised considerations.

"A Saile!"

"How beares she," or "stands shee, to wind-ward or lee-ward? Set him by the Compasse!"

"He stands right ahead," or, "on the weather-Bow," or, "lee-Bow."

Let flie your colours if you have a consort, else not. "Out with all your sailes! A Steady man to the helme! *To give chase.* Sit close to keepe her steady. Give him chase," or, "Fetch him up! Hee holds his owne—no, we gather on him!"

76

"Captaine, out goes his flag and pendants [pennants], also his *waste clothes* and *top armings*!"; which is a long red cloth, about three quarters of a yard broad, edged on each side with Calico or white linnen cloth, that goeth round about the ship on the out sides of all her upper workes fore and aft, and before the cubbridge heads; also, about the fore and [60] maine tops, as well for the countenance and grace of the ship as to cover the men for being seene.

Wast [waist] clothes.

Top armings.

Hee furles and slings his maine yard, in goes his spret-saile. Thus they use to strip themselves into their *short sailes* or *fig[h]ting sailes*, which is onely the fore saile, the maine and fore-top sailes, because the rest should not be fired nor spoiled. Besides, they would be troublesome to handle, hinder our sights, and the using our armes.

Fighting sailes.
To hale a ship.

He makes ready his close fights fore and aft.
"Master, how stands the chase?"
"Right on head, I say."
"Well, we shall reatch him by and by. What's, all ready?"
"Yea, yea!"
"Every man to his charge! Dowse your top-saile to salute him for the Sea! Haile him with a noise of trumpets! . . . Whence is your ship?"
"Of *Spaine*! Whence is yours?"
"Of *England*! Are you a Merchant, or a man of War?"
"We are of the Sea!" He waves us to lee-ward with his drawne sword, cals amaine[1] for the King of *Spaine*, and springs his loufe.[2]
"Give him a chase peece with your broad side, and run a good berth ahead of him!"
"Done, done!"

How to begin a fight.

[1] Mainwaring, *op. cit.*, II, 87 : *waving amaine* : "to make a sign to them that they should strike their topsail [as a sign of surrender]."
[2] *Ibid.*, 182, "When a ship is going large, to clap close by a wind [to turn to the windward]."

"We have the wind of him, and he tackes about. Tack you about also and keepe your loufe. Be yare at the helme! Edge in with him, give him a volley of a small shot, also your prow and broade side as before, and keep your loufe!"

He payes us shot for shot. Well, wee shall requite him.

"What, are you ready againe?"

"Yea, yea!"

"Try him once more as before!"

"Done, done!"

"Keepe your loufe and loge [load] your ordnance againe. Is all ready?"

"Yea, yea!"

"Edge in with him againe, begin with your bow peeces, proceed with your broad side, & let her fall off with the wind, to give her also your full chase, your weather broad side, and bring her round that the sterne may also discharge, and your tackes close aboord againe!

"Done, done!"

The wind veeres, the Sea goes too high to boord her, and wee are shot thorow and thorow, and *betweene wind and water*.[1] "Try the pump! Beare up the helme!"

How to sling a man over boord. "Master, let us breathe and refresh a little, and sling a man over boord to stop the leakes." That is, to trusse him up about the middle in a peece of canvas, and a rope to keepe him from sinking, and his armes at liberty; with a malet in the one hand, & a plug lapped in Okum and [61] well-tarred in a tarpawling clout in the other, which he will quickly beat into the hole or holes the bullets made.

"What cheere mates, is all well?"

"All well, all well, all well!"

Then make ready to beare up with him againe, and

[1] Holed through in that space between the water line when the ship is upright, and the water line when the ship is heeled over in the wind at sea. A ship holed through *between wind and water* on the starboard side while on a starboard tack, cannot come about until the hole has been plugged.

with all your great and small shot charge him, and in the smoke boord him thwart the hawse, on the bow, mid ships, or rather then saile, on his quarter; or make fast your graplings if you can to his close fights, and sheare off.

"Captaine, we are fowle on each other, and the ship is on fire!"

Cut any thing to get cleare, and smother the fire with wet cloathes. In such a case they will presently be such friends, as to help one the other all they can to get cleare, lest they both should burne together and sinke; and if they be generous, the fire quenched, drinke kindely one to another, heave their cans over boord, and then begin againe as before.

"Well, Master, the day is spent, the night drawes on, let us consult. Chirurgion, looke to the wounded and winde up the slaine, with each a weight or bullet at their heads and feet to make them sinke, and give them three gunnes for their funerals. Swabber, make cleane the ship. Purser, record their Names. Watch, be vigilant to keepe your berth to wind ward that we lose him not in the night. Gunners, spunge your Ordnance. Souldiers, scowre your peeces. Carpenters, about your leakes. Boatswaine and the rest, repaire the sailes and shrouds, and Cooke, see you observe your directions against the morning watch. Boy!"

A consultation & direction in a sea fight, & how they bury their dead.

"Holla, Master, Holla!"

"Is the kettle boiled?"

"Yea, yea!"

"Boatswaine, call up the men to prayer and breakefast."

"Boy, fetch my cellar of bottls. A health to you all, fore and aft, courage, my hearts, for a fresh charge! Gunners, beat open the ports and out with your lower tire [tier], and bring me from the weather side to the lee so many peeces as we have ports to beare upon him.

A preparation for a fresh charge.

79

Master, lay him aboord loufe for loufe. Mid ships men, see the tops and yards well manned, with stones, fire pots and brasse bailes [balls, see p. 87] to throw amongst them before we enter, or if we be put off, charge them with all your great and small shot. In the smoke let us enter [62] them in the shrouds, and every squadron at his best advantage. So sound Drums and Trumpets, and Saint *George* for England![1]"

How a prise doth veeld, and how to entertaine him Sea-man like.

They hang out a flag of truce. Hale him a-maine, a-base, or take in his flag, strike their sailes, and come aboord with their Captaine, Purser and Gunner, with their commission, cocket,[2] or bils of loading. Out goes the boat, they are lanched from the ship side. Entertaine them with a generall cry, "God save the Captaine and all the company!," with the Trumpets sounding. Examine them in particular, and then conclude your conditions with feasting, freedome or punishment, as you find occasion; but alwayes have as much care to their wounded as your owne, and if there be either young women or aged men, use them nobly, which is ever the nature of a generous disposition. To conclude, if you surprize him, or enter perforce, you may stow the men, rifle, pillage or sacke, and cry a prise.[3]

How to call a Counsell of War, and order a Navy at Sea.

To call a Councell of Warre in a Fleet: there is your Councell of Warre to manage all businesses of import, and the common Councell for matters of small moment. When they would have a meeting—(where the Admirall doth appoint it), if in the Admirall [flag-ship], they hang out a flag in the maine shrouds; if in the Vice Admirall, in the fore shrouds; if in the Reare Admirall, in the mizen.

---

[1] It was the Cross of St. George that was flown at the foretop of English ships of the period.

[2] A custom house certificate indicating that the duty on merchandise aboard has been paid.

[3] Claim them as a prize under conditions layed down by Admiralty law.

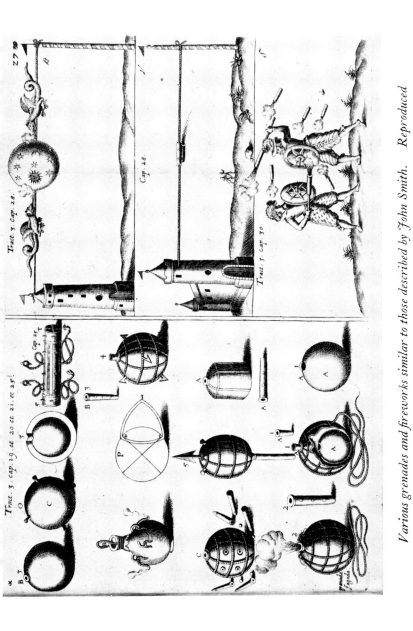

Various grenades and fireworks similar to those described by John Smith. Reproduced from The Gunner *by Robert Norton (1628)*

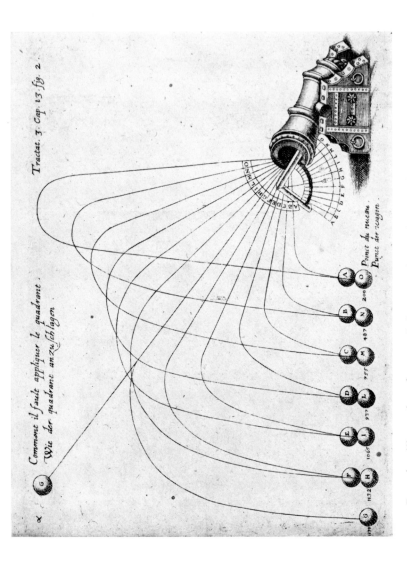

Drawing illustrating the use of the gunner's quadrant. Reproduced from The Gunner *by Robert Norton (1628)*

If there bee many squadrons, the Admirall of each squadron, upon sundry occasions, doth carry in their maine tops flags of sundry colours, or else they are distinguished by severall pendants from the yards' armes. Every night or morning they are to come under the Lee of the Admirall to salute him and know his pleasure, but no Admirall of any squadron is to beare his flag in the maine top in the presence of the Admirall generall, except the Admirall come aboord of him to Councell, to dinner, or collation; and so any ship else where he so resideth during that time, is to weare his flag in the maine top.

They use to martiall or order those squadrons in rankes like Manaples,[1] which is foure square, if the wind and Sea permits—a good berth or distance from [63] each other, that they becalme not one another, nor come not fowle of each other; the Generall commonly in the middest, his Vice Admirall in the front, and his Reare Admirall in the Reare. Or otherwise like a halfe Moone, which is two squadrons like two triangles for the two hornes, and so the rest of the squadrons behinde each other a good distance, and the Generall in the middest of the halfe circle, from whence he seeth all his fleet and sendeth his directions as he findes occasion, to whom he pleaseth.

Now betweene two Navies they use often, especially in a harbour or road where they are at anchor, to fill old Barkes with pitch, tar, traine [whale] oile, lincet [linseed] oile, brimstone [sulphur], rosen, reeds, with dry wood and such combustible things; sometimes they linke three or foure together in the night, and puts them adrift as they finde occasion.

Stratagems for Sea-men.

To passe a fort, some will make both ship and sailes all black. But if the fort keepe but a fire on the other side,

[1] Formations consisting of small squads of footsoldiers.

H

81

and all the peeces point blanke with the fire, if they discharge [at] what is betwixt them and the fire, the shot will hit if the rule bee truly observed; for when a ship is betwixt the fire and you, she doth keepe you from seeing it till shee bee past it.[1]

To conclude, there is as many stratagems, advantages and inventions to be used as you finde occasions, and therefore experience must be the best Tutor.[2]

[1] William Bourne, *The Art of Shooting*, p. 92 (see p. 90 f.n., below).
[2] Robert Norton, *The Gunner*, Sig. B verso (see p. xiii).

Chapter XIV

The names of all sorts of great Ordnance, and their appurtenances, with their proper tearmes and expositions, also divers observations concerning their shooting, with a Table of proportion for their weight of metall, weight of powder, weight of shot, and there best at randome and point blanke inlarged.

A Canon royal, or double Canon; a Canon, a Canon Serpentine, a bastard Canon, a demy Canon, a Canon Petro; a Culvering, a Basilisco, a demy culvering, a bastard Culvering; a Sacar [Saker], a Minion, a Falcon, a Falconet, a Serpentine, a Rabbinet.[1] *The Names of great Ordnance.*

To all those doe belong *Carriages*, whereon peeces [cannon] doe lie, supported by an axeltree betwixt two wheeles; whereon doth lie the peece upon her *Trunnions*, which are two knobs cast with the peece on each of her sides, which doth lie in two halfe holes upon the two cheekes of the carriages, to raise her up or downe as you will. Over them are the *Capsquares*, which are two broad peeces of iron [which] doth cover them, made fast by a pin with a fore locke to keepe the peece from falling out. *Carriages.* *Trunnions.* *Capsquares.*

That the peece and carriages is drawne along upon *wheeles*, every one doth know. If shee bee for land service, *Wheeles.*

[1] The spelling of these varies.

they have wheeles made with spokes like coach wheeles, and according to their proportion, strongly shod with iron; and [65] the pins at the ends of the Axeltree is called *Linch pins*.

Trucks.
To mount a
Peece.
To dismount a
Peece.
Beds.
Quoines.

If for Sea, she have *Trucks*, which are round, intier [entire] peeces of wood like wheeles. *To mount a peece* is to lay her upon her carriages; *to dismount* her, to take her downe. Her *Bed* is a planke [which] doth lie next the peece, or the peece upon it upon the carriage; and betwixt the Peece and it they put their *Quoines*, which are great wedges of wood with a little handle at the end, to put them forward or backward for levelling the Peece as you please. To *travas* a Peece is to turne her which way you will upon her Platforme.

Travas
[traverse].
Dispert [dispart].
Britch [breech].
Carnouse.[1]
Musell [muzzle].

To *dispert* a Peece is to find a difference betwixt the thicknesse of the metall at her mouth and *britch*, or *carnouse*, which is the greatest circle about her britch (and her *musell Ring* is the greatest circle about her mouth), thereby to make a just shot. There are divers waies to dispert her, but the most easiest is as good as the best, and that is but by putting a little sticke or a straw that is strait [straight] into the toutch hole to the lower part of the *Sillinder* or *Concave*, which is the *Bore* of the Peece, and cut it off close by the metall; and then apply it in the same manner to the mouth, and it will exactly shew you the difference. Which being set upon the mussell of the Peece with a little Clay, Pitch or Wax, it will bee as the pin of any Peece is to the sight—levell to the carnouse or britch of the Peece; otherwaies you may give her allowance according to your judgement.[2]

Sillender
[cylinder].
Concave.
Bore.
How to dispert
a Peece.

Taper boared
[bored].

Taper boared is when a peece is wider at the mouth then towards the britch, which is dangerous (if the Bullet goe not home) to burst her.

[1] The *carnouze* was the French term which was known to Smith through his experience but was not mentioned by Bourne or Norton.
[2] This follows Norton's description (*ibid.* 66) more closely than Bourne's.

84

Honicombed is when shee is ill cast or overmuch worne, shee will bee rugged [rough] within, which is dangerous for a crosse barre shot to catch hold by, or any ragge of her wadding, being a fire and sticking there, may fire the next charge you put in her; and you may finde if she be Taper boarded [sic: honey combed] either with a crooked wyer [wire] at the end of a long staffe, by scratching up and downe to see where you can catch any hold; or a light candle at the end of a staffe, thrust up and down, to see if you can see any fault.

Britchings are the ropes by which you lash your Ordnance [66] fast to the Ship's side in foule weather.

Chambers is a charge made of brasse or iron which we use to put in at the britch of a sling or Murtherer, containing just so much powder as will drive away the case of stones, or shot, or any thing in her. In a great Peece we call that her Chamber so far as the powder doth reach when she is laded [loaded].

A *Cartrage* is a bagge of Canvasse made upon a frame or a round peece of wood, somewhat less than the bore of the Peece. They make them also of paper. They have also Cartrages, or rather cases for Cartrages, made of Lattin [see p. 10] to keepe the Cartrages in, which is to have no more powder in them than just the charge of your Peece; and they are closely covered in those *cases* of Latten to keepe them dry and from any mischances by fire, and are farrer more ready and safer than your Ladles or Budgbarrels. A *Budgbarrell* is a little Barrell made of Latten, filled with powder, to carry from place to place, for feare of fire. In the cover it hath a long necke to fill the Ladles withall without opening.

A *Ladle* is a long staffe with a peece of thin Copper at the end like halfe a Cartrage, in bredth and length so much as will hold no more powder than the due charge for the Peece it belongs to. A *Spunge* is such another

Hon[e]y-combed.

How to finde it.

Britchings [breechings].

Chambers.

Cartrages [cartridges].

Cases.

Budg[e]barell.

A Ladle.

A Spunge [sponge].

85

staffe, with a peece of a Lambe skin at the end about it, to thrust up and downe the Peece, to take off the dust, moisture, or sparkes of fire if any remaine in her. And a *A Rammer.* *Rammer* is a bob of wood at the other end, to ramme home *Waddings.* the Powder and the Waddings. *Waddings* is Okum, old clouts [rags], or straw, put [in] after the powder and the Bullet.

Wood Cases. A *Case* is made of two peeces of hollow wood joined together like two halfe cartrages, fit to put into the bore of *Case shot.* a Peece; & a *Case Shot* is any kinde of small Bullets, Nailes, old iron or the like, to put into the case, to shoot out of the Ordnances or Murderers. These will doe much mischiefe when wee lie boord and boord; but for Spunges and Rammers they use now a stiffe Rope a little more than the length of the Peece, which you may turne and wind within boord as you will with much more ease and safety than the other. [67]

Round shot. *Round Shot* is a round Bullet for any Peece. *Cros-* *Crosse bar shot.* *barshot* is also a round shot, but it hath a long spike of Iron cast with it as if it did goe thorow the middest of it, *To Arme a shot.* the ends whereof are commonly *armed* for feare of bursting the Peece; which is to binde a little Okum in a *Trundle shot.* little Canvasse at the end of each Pike [spike]. *Trundle shot* is onely a bolt of iron sixteene or eighteene inches in length, at both ends sharpe pointed, and about a handfull from each end, a round broad bowle of lead, according *Langrill* to the bore of the Peece cast upon it. Langrell shot runnes *[langrel] shot.* loose with a shackell, to be shortened when you put it into the Peece, and when it flies out it doth spred it selfe. It hath at the end of either barre a halfe Bullet either of *Chaine shot.* lead or iron. *Chaine shot* is two bullets with a chaine betwixt them, and some are contrived round, as in a ball, yet will spred in flying their full length in bredth.

All these are used when you are neere a ship, to shoot downe Masts, Yards, Shrouds, teare the sailes, spoile the men, or any thing that is above the decks.

86

Fire-workes are divers, and of many compositions, as *Arrowes trimmed with wild fire,*[1] to sticke in the sailes or ship's side, shot burning. *Pikes of wild fire,* to strike burning into a ship side to fire her. There is also divers sorts of *Granados,* some to breake and fly in abundance of peeces every way, as will your brasse balls, and earthen pots, which when they are covered with quartered bullets stucke in pitch, and the pots filled with good powder, in a crowd of people will make an incredible slaughter. Some will burne under water, and never extinguish till the stuffe bee consumed; some onely will burne and fume out a most stinking poison smoke; some, being but onely an Oile, being [an-]nointed on any thing made of dry wood, will take fire by the heat of the Sunne when the Sunne shines hot [phosphorus]. There is also a Powder, which being laid in like manner upon any thing subject to burne, will take fire if either any raine or water light upon it [sodium].

But those inventions are bad on shore, but much worse at Sea, and are naught because so dangerous, and not easie to bee quenched; and their practise worse, because they may doe [68] as much mischiefe to a friend as to an enemy, therfore I will leave them as they are.

There are also divers sorts of *Powder.* The *Serpentine* is like dust and weake, and will not keepe at Sea, but be[-come] moist. The common sort is *great corned powder,* but grosse, and onely used in great Ordnance. Your *fine corned Powder,* for hand Guns, is in goodnesse as your Salt-Peter is oft refined, and from ten pence a pound to eighteene pence a pound.

A *Tomkin* is a round peece of wood put into the Peece's-mouth and covered with Tallow,[2] and a *Fid,* a little Okum made like a naile, put in at the toutch hole and covered

Fire workes.
Arrowes of wild fire.
Pikes of wild fire.
Granados [grenades] of divers sorts.
Brasse Balles.

Powder.
Serpentine powder.
Grosse corned Powder.
Fine corned Powder.
A Tomkin [tampkin].
A Fid.

[1] A mixture of sulphur, naphtha and pitch.
[2] To keep out the rain and sea water.

87

with a thin lead bound above it, to keepe the Powder dry in the Peece.

Shackels **[shackles].**

Shackels are a kinde of Rings, but not round, made like them at the hatches cornee[r]s (by which we take them up and lay them downe) but bigger, fixed to the middest of the ports within boord; through which wee put a billet to keepe fast the port for flying open in foule weather, which may easily indanger, if not sinke the Ship.

To cloy a Peece or poyson her.
To uncloy.

To *Cloy* or *Poison* a Peece is to drive a naile into her toutch hole; then you cannot give fire. And to *Uncloy* her is to put as much oile as you can about the naile to make it glib, and by a traine give fire to her by her mouth, and so blow it out.

Compasse Callipers.

Compasse Callipers belongs to the Gunner, and is like two halfe Circles that hath a handle and joint like a paire of Compasses, but they are blunt at the points, to open as you please for to dispert a Peece. A *Horne* is his touch box;[1] his *Primer* is a small long peece of iron, sharpe at the small end, to pierce the Cartrage thorow the toutch hole. His *Lint stock* is a handsome carved stick, more than halfe a yard long, with a Cocke at the one end to hold fast his Match, and a sharpe pike [spike] in the other to sticke it fast upon the Deck or platforme upright.

Horne.
Priming Iron.

Lint stocke.

Gunner's quadrant.
Darke Lanthorn [lantern].
Morters [mortars].
The names of small Peeces, and their implements.

The *Gunner's quadrant* is to levell a Peece, or mount her to any random. A *darke Lanthorne* is as well to be used by any body as he.

For *Morters*, or such chambers as are only used for triumphs, there is no use for them in this service; but for *currjours*,[2] *Hargabusacrocks* [arquebus à croc], [69] *Muskets*, *Bastard-muskets*, *Colivers* [caliver], *Crabuts*, *Carbin[e]s*, *long Pistols* or *short Pistols*, there belongs to

[1] A container for touch or priming powder.
[2] A currier was the same caliber as an arquebus, but had a longer barrel. An arquebus à croc was fired from a rest with a fork or crotch (croc) at the top. These were rarely used at sea, since using a rest on a rolling deck was difficult. The musket of the day was a heavy gun designed to be fired from the shoulder, or with the aid of

them *Bandiliers*, *bullet Bags*, *Wormes*, *Scowrers*, *melting Ladles*, *Lead*, *Molds* of al sorts to cast their shot.

Quarter Bullets is but any bullet quartered in foure or eight parts, and all those are as usefull a ship-boord as on shore.

For the soule,[1] trunke, bore, fortification, the diversity of their metals, and divers other curious Theormes or tearmes used about great Ordnance, there are so many uncertainties as well in her mounting, levelling upon her platforme, as also the accidents that may happen in the powder, the ground, the aire, and differences in proportion, [that] I will not undertake to prescribe any certaine artificiall rule. These proportions following are neere the matter, but for your better satisfaction reade Master Digs' *Pantrimetria*,[2] Master Smith,[3] or Master

Bandilers [bandaleers].
Bullet bags.
Wormes.
Scowrers.
Melting Ladles.
Lead Molds.
Quartered shot.

a rest. The bastard musket was lighter in caliber, about .69. A caliver was a heavy arquebus, but fired from the shoulder.

The crabut was Smith's Anglicized version of the crapaudeau or crapaudine, a French breech-loading swivel gun, similar to a murderer, that he had come across in his life as a journeyman soldier. A carbine was a short-barrelled gun used by horsemen, also in close quarters at sea.

The editor wishes to express his indebtedness to Harold L. Peterson, Chief Curator of the National Park Service, Washington, D.C., the author of many fine books on ancient armament, for his help with the above passages.

[1] Norton, *The Gunner, ibid.*, page 128: "The hollow concave, cillinder or bore of the peece may be called the soule . . ."

[2] Leonard Digges (completed by his son, Thomas), *A Geometrical practise named Pantometria* (1571, 1591). This was a book of instruction in plane and solid geometry, surveying and map-making. It gives one of the first descriptions of the telescope. The word "theodolite" appears for the first time. It is not a book on gunnery, yet the systems it gives for plotting angles, distances and elevations were also necessary in aiming cannon. If Smith had indeed absorbed the material in this book, he would have been technically equipped to make the maps that are attributed to him. His authorship of the Chesapeake Bay map has often been questioned.

[3] Sir John Smythe, *Certain Discourses concerning the forms and effect of divers sorts of Weapons* (1590); also, *Instructions, observations and orders Mylitary* (1595). Smythe was an expert in all types of weapons and military tactics. He must have been regarded as a shell-back by the younger men, since he favoured the longbow and even the crossbow over guns in battle.

Burnes' *Art of Gunnery*,[1] or Master Robert Norton's[2] *Exposition upon Master Digs' Stratiaticos*.[3] Any of those will show the Theoricke at large. But to bee a good Gunner, you must learne it by practise.[4]

[70] Table of ordinance—facsimile[5] (facing page 64).

[71]

Note that seldome in Ships [do] they use any Ordnance greater than Demy Canons, nor have they any certainty either at point blanke or any random.

Note your Serpentine powder in old time was in meale, but now corned and made stronger, and called *Canon corne powder*.[6]

But that for small Ordnance is called *corne Powder fine*, and ought to have in strength a quarter more, because those small Peeces are better fortified than the greater.

---

[1] William Bourne, *The Arte of shooting in Great Ordnaunce* (1587). Smith used a few items from Bourne, although he appears to have leaned more heavily on Norton.

[2] Robert Norton, *Of the Art of Great Artillery, viz. The Explanation of the most excellent and necessary Definitions and Questions, pronounced and propounded by that rare Souldier and Mathematician*, Thomas Digges, *Esquire; and by him published, in his Stratiotics and Pantometria, concering great Ordinaunces, and his Theorems thereupon* (1624). Norton had written a congratulatory verse in Smith's *The Generall Historie of Virginia, New England and the Summer Isles*, also written in 1624. In turn, Smith wrote a verse for Norton's *The Gunner*, 1628, which is reproduced on page xiii.

[3] Thomas Digges, *An arithmeticall Militare Treatise named Stratioticos* (1579, 1590).
Digges was Muster Master-General of the British forces in the Low Countries. The book begins with a basic course in arithmetic and algebra, and other mathematics, as they apply to the military. It gives the duties of soldiers and officers, also military laws and regulations in the Low Countries circa 1586.

[4] Norton, *The Gunner*, page 10.

[5] This table is similar to, but not identical with the table in *The Gunner*, page 53. It may possibly have been taken from the copy of Mainwaring's *Nomenclature Navalis* mentioned in the *Sea Grammar*'s preface, page xiii.

[6] Norton, *The Gunner*, page 53.

Now if you have but one sort of Powder for all, abate
$\frac{1}{4}$ part, and cut off $\frac{1}{4}$ of the bredth and length of your
Ladle.

But Cartrages are now found the best and most
readiest.[1]

Provided alwaies, that all Shot must be a quarter [of an
inch][2] lesse than the height of the Peece.

[1] Bourne, *Art of Shooting*, page 31
[2] Norton, *op. cit.*, page 95.

Chapter XV

How they divide their shares in a man of Warre; what Bookes and Instruments are fit for a Sea-man; with divers advertisements for Sea men; and the use of the petty Tally.

The ship hath one third part, the victuallar the other third, the other third part is for the Company, and this *Shares.* is subdivided thus in *shares*.

The Captaine hath — 10 ————————in some but 9.
The Lieutenant – 9 ... or as he agreeth with the Captaine.
The Master ———— 8 ————————in some but 7.
The Mates ———— 7 ——————————— 5.
The Chirurgion —— 6 ——————————— 3.
The Gunner———— 6 ——————————— 5.
The Boatswaine —— 6 ——————————— 5.
The Carpenter ——— 6 ——————————— 5.
The Trumpeter ——— 6 ——————————— 5.
The 4. quarter Mast. 5 – apeece, or——————— 4.
The Cooper ———— 5 ——————————— 4.
The Chirurg. Mate—— 5 ——————————— 4.
The Gunners Mate—— 5 ——————————— 4.
The Carpent. Mate—— 5 ——————————— 4.
The Corporall ——— 4 ——————————— 3.
The quarter Gunners – 4 ——————————— 3.

continued on next page.

¹ Pagination skips from 72 to 83. This is a printer's error.

The Trump. Mate —— 3	————————	3½.
The Steward———— 4	————————	3.
The Cooke ———— 4	————————	3.
The Coxswaine ——— 4	————————	3.
The Swabber ——— 4	————————	3.

[83]

In English ships they seldome use any Marshall, whose shares amongst the French is equall with the Boatswaine's; all the rest of the Younkers or foremast men, according to their deserts; some 3, some 2 and ½, some 1 and ½, and the boyes 1, which is a single share, or 1 and ½, or as they doe deserve.

Now the Master, or his right hand Mate, the Gunner, Boatswaine and foure quarter Masters doe make the shares, not the Captaine, who hath onely this privilege: to take away halfe a share, or a whole share at most, to give from one to another as he best pleaseth.

For to learne to observe the Altitude, Latitude, Longitude, Amplitude, the variation of the Compasse, the Sun's Azimuth and Almicanter;[1] to shift the Sunne and Moone[2], and know the tides, your Roomes [rhumbs,][3] pricke your Card,[4] say your Compasse, and get some of these bookes; but practice is the best.

---

1 Almacantar: an obsolete Spanish term, of Arabic derivation, for parallels of altitude. When two stars are in the same almacantar, they have the same altitude.

2 In *The Seaman's Secrets*, 1599 edition, B4 verso—C2 (see below), John Davis described an instrument, a "Horizontal Tide Table, whereby he may shift the sun or moon." By this, high tide in any given place could be ascertained if the bearings were known, and the "age" of the moon. Also, see Bourne, *Sea Regiment* (see below), 1596 edition, page 11 verso.

3 Rhumbs or Rhumblines are lines that intersect meridians at the same angle. The rhumb would be the ship's course.

4 To lay out the ship's position and course upon the sea-chart.

Master *Wright's* errours of Navigation.[1]

Master *Tapp's* Sea-mans' Kalender.[2]

The Art of Navigation.[3]

The Sea Regiment.[4]

The Sea-man's secret.[5]

Waggoner.[6]

Master *Gunter's* workes.[7]

The Sea-man's glasse for the Scale.[8]

The New Attracter for variation.[9]

Master *Wright* for use of the Globe.[10]

Master *Hewes* [Hughes] for the same.[11]

---

[1] Edward Wright (1558–1615), *Certaine Errors of Navigation Revealed*. Written in 1592, published 1599, 1610. For this and other books following, see David M. Waters, *The Art of Navigation in England in Elizabethan and Early Stuart Times*, New Haven, 1958.

[2] John Tapp (fl. 1596–1615), *The Seamans's Kalendar*, 1602. It was revised about every three years. By 1631, 10 editions had appeared.

[3] Martin Cortes, *Arte de Navegar* (1551, Seville), translated by Richard Eden, *The Arte of Navigation* (1561); reprinted 1572, 1579, 1589. Enlarged by John Tapp, 1596; reprinted 1609, 1615, 1630.

[4] William Bourne, *A Regiment for the Sea*, 1574, 1576, 1577, 1580. Edited by Thomas Hood, 1592, with at least six more editions through 1631.

[5] John Davis (1552–1605), *The Seaman's Secrets* (1594); reprinted 1599, etc.

[6] Lucas Janszoon Wagenaer, *Spiegel der Zeevaert*, 1584, 1585. Translated into English by Anthony Ashley (1588), under the title *The Mariner's Mirrour*.

[7] Edmund Gunter (1581–1626), *Description and use of Sector. The Cross staff, and other Instruments*, 1623; second imprint, 1624.

[8] John Aspley, *Speculum Nauticum, a looking-glass for Sea-men* (1624).

[9] Robert Norman (1560–1596), *The New Attractive*, 1581, 1585, 1596, 1614 etc.

[10] Edward Wright, *Description and Use of the Sphere*, (1613), and later editions, including one in 1627.

[11] Robert Hues (1553–1632), *Tractatus de Globis* (1594); Dutch edition, 1597; French, 1623; first edition in English, 1628. This was written for use with Emery Molyneaux's globe. It is possible that Smith saw the manuscript of this book as he did Noron's *The Gunner*, also published in 1628.

Instruments fitting for a Sea-man.

Compasses, so many paire and sorts as you will; an Astrolobe Quadrant,[1] a Crossestaffe,[2] a Backe staffe,[3] an Astrolobe,[4] a Nocturnall.[5] [84]

Young Gentlemen that desires command at Sea ought well to consider the condition of his ship, victuall and company; for if there be more learners than sailers, how slightly soever many esteeme sailers, all the worke to save ship, goods and lives must lie upon them, especially

Advertisements [advice] for young Commanders, Captaines, and other officers.

[1] This was the astrolabe in its simplest form—an instrument for measuring vertical angles, using gravity to get a vertical reference rather than the horizon, like the backstaff and cross staff. The true astrolabe had the altitude measuring device on one side, but on the opposite side is the RETE, with selected star positions, and inside are a number of plates with stereographic projections for different latitudes. These provided a graphical solution of the spherical triangle. (See plate, facing page 65.)
The editor takes this opportunity of thanking Frederick W. Keator, Planetarium Director at Mystic Seaport Museum, Mystic, Connecticut, for his generous aid and information concerning these instruments.
[2] An instrument used for sighting the angle of the sun or other heavenly bodies with the horizon or with each other, for determining latitude. Its use was limited to the middle latitudes, and the star sights had to be made at dawn or sunset, when the star and the horizon were both visible.
[3] This was invented by John Davis. The observer stood with his back to the sun, and the reading was made by sighting along the staff at the horizon. The cross-arm was moved until the shadow of the arm hit a slot that lined up with the horizon (see plate, facing page 65). This was far superior because the observer did not have to look into the sun, and the shadow of the sun and the horizon were brought together on a point, so that it was not necessary to sight on two things at once.
This was later improved by Davis and Wright into the quadrant, which utilized the same principal, but was more accurate and had wider applications.
[4] The astrolabe was also used to ascertain latitude and time by measuring the altitude of heavenly bodies. It differed from the above instruments in that it used gravity to give a reference line from which angles were measured, using a plumb bob, or its own weight, when hung from a finger. It was hard to manage in a rough sea, but it could be used at night for star sights.
[5] An instrument used for determining latitude by observing the Pole Star.

95

in fowle weather. Then their labour, hazzard, wet and cold is so incredible, I cannot expresse it. It is not then the number of them that here can say at home, "What I cannot doe I can quickly learne," and, "What a great matter is it to saile a ship, or goe to Sea." Surely those for a good time will doe more trouble than good. I confesse it is most necessary such should goe, but not too many in one ship; for if the labour of threescore should lie upon thirty (as many times it doth), they are so over-charged with labour, bruises and overstraining themselves, they fall sick of one disease or other; for there is on dallying nor excuses with stormes, gusts, over-growne Seas and lee-shores, and when their victuall is putrified it endangers all. Men of all other professions, in lightning, thunder, stormes, and tempests with raine and snow, may shelter themselves in dry houses by good fires; but those are the chiefe times Sea-men must stand to their tackling, and attend with all diligence their greatest labour upon the deckes.

Many suppose any thing is good enough to serve men at sea, and yet nothing sufficient for them ashore, either for their healthes, for their ease, or estates, or state. A Commander at Sea should doe well to thinke the contary, and provide for himselfe and company in like manner; also seriously to consider what will bee his charge to furnish himselfe at Sea with bedding, linnen, armes and apparrell, how to keepe his table aboord, and his expences on shore, and provide his petty Tally, which is a competent proportion according to your number of these particulars following:

The petty Tally. Fine wheat flower, close and well packed; Rice, Currands [currants], Sugar, Prunes, Cynamon, Ginger, Pepper, Cloves, greene Ginger; Oyle, Butter, Holland cheese or [85] old Cheese; Wine vineger, Canarie sacke, *Aqua vitæ*, the best Wines, the best waters, the juyce [juice] of Limons [lemons] for the scurvy; white Bisket,

Oatmeale, gammons of Bacon, dried Neats' tongues; Beefe packed up in vineger [pickled]; Legs of Mutton, minced and stewed and close packed up with tried sewet [boiled suet] or butter in earthen pots. To entertaine strangers, Marmalad, Suckets [fruit preserves], Almonds, Comfits[1] and such like.

The use of the petty Tally.

Some it may be will say I would have men rather to feast than fight; but I say, the want of those necessaries occasions the losse of more men than in any English fleet hath beene slaine since 88 [the Spanish Armada]. For when a man is ill or at the point of death, I would know whether a dish of buttered Rice with a little Cynamon, Ginger and Sugar, a little minced meat or rost Beefe, a few stewed Prunes, a race [root] of greene Ginger, a Flap-jacke, a can of fresh Water brewed with a little Cinamon, Ginger and Sugar—bee not better than a little poore John [hard dried cod], or salt fish with oile and mustard; or bisket, butter, cheese or oatmeale pottage on fish dayes; or on flesh dayes, salt Beefe, Porke and Pease with six shillings beere.

This is your ordinary ship's allowance, and good for them [that] are well, if well conditioned, which is not alwayes, as Sea-men can (too well) witnesse. And after a storme, when poore men are all wet, and some have not so much as a cloth to shift [change] him, shaking with cold—few of those but wil tell you a little Sacke or *Aqua vitæ* is much better to keepe them in health than a little small beere, or cold water, although it be sweet.

Now that every one should provide those things for himselfe, few of them have either that providence or meanes; and there is neither Ale-house, Taverne nor Inne to burne a faggot in, neither Grocer, Poulterer, Apothecary nor Butcher's shop, and therefore the use of this petty Tally is necessary, and thus to be imploied as there is occasion. To entertaine strangers as they are in

---

[1] Sugar-preserved fruits or roots; confiture or preserves.

quality, every Commander should shew himselfe as like himselfe as he can, as well for the credit of the ship and his setters-forth [86] as himselfe; but in that herein every one may moderate themselves according to their owne pleasures, therefore I leave it to their own discretions; and this briefe discourse, and my selfe, to their friendly construction, and good opinion.

FINIS.

INDEX